life-changing principles for pre-marriage relationships

ROMANCE
GOD'S WAY

ERIC & LESLIE LUDY

MAKARIOS
PUBLISHING INC.
LONGMONT, COLORADO

Makarios Publishing Inc.
3119 Concord Way
Longmont, Colorado 80503

"I Surrender My Will," page 74, copyright © 1996 Laura Hart.

ISBN 0-9656251-0-9
Printed in the United States of America

To Leslie,
my Princess of Purity . . .
Thank you for tenderly displaying to me
what it means to love with your life.

Eric

To Eric,
my Knight in Shining Armor . . .
Thank you for building me
a castle of dreams.

Leslie

For I know the plans
I have for you,
says the Lord.
They are plans for good
and not for evil,
to give you a future and a hope.

Jeremiah 29:11 TLB

CONTENTS

ACKNOWLEDGEMENTS

Special thanks to Richard Runkles
for making this project possible,

to Mark Ludy for his hilarious creativity,

and to Marlene Bagnull
for patiently and diligently working
to strengthen this message.

Most of all,
thank you to the true Author
of anything worthwhile within these pages.
To Him be the glory!

FOREWORD

I first met Eric and Leslie on their 1996 Australian tour while interviewing them for a television program. I was immediately enthusiastic about their message and the timeliness of their ministry. I am excited to heartily recommend their new book to anyone looking for godly wisdom in the area of relationships, for I believe the message within it signals a turning point for today's youth.

The book you are about to read will delight and inspire you! Eric and Leslie have poured their talents and personalities into these pages along with personal glimpses of their individual journeys and a clear vision of sowing living seed into your heart.

The message of *Romance God's Way* is a message of hope. For many young people, families, and leaders "hope" has been buried in the ashes of burned out dreams. But Eric and Leslie are living proof that a better way not only exists but has been walked out successfully.

This is not a sentimental workout for the emotionally vulnerable. These pages have been carved out of personal experience, prayerful insight, faithful obedience, and deep

longing for reality. The result is a book filled with clear, abundant wisdom about how to re-think, reclaim, and revitalize vision for a godly and glorious future. Humor, anecdotes, illustrations, and street-smart reality bring the truth of Scripture to ready grasp.

Eric and Leslie are 100% sincere, absolutely real, genuinely concerned about you, sensitively in love with the Lord, and enriched in their own relationship by mining the treasure of·God's better way.

This material has been presented many times across the United States and Australia. The teaching has been tested and approved by youth from all kinds of backgrounds. I know of no one else who has drawn these truths together so powerfully. A unique couple have created a unique presentation! And their heart's desire is that this message grip you, liberate you, and set you on your own wonderful journey so you too can have a message for the nations.

Don't let the world's pattern of pain pull you down any longer. This unique message will turn your life around and plant in you seeds to the sweetest happiness and the greatest satisfaction. Read on with open hearts. Read with confidence and be ready to apply the truth with faith-filled commitment. Read on and be transformed!

Chris Field
Melbourne, Victoria, Australia

Chris Field is an Australian pastor and television personality. He presents two weekly TV programs in the City·of Melbourne, Victoria—a Bible teaching program, "Living Word," and an interview program, "Melbourne Alive." Chris has five sons and a daughter and ministers widely on family, marriage, personal wholeness, and applying Scripture to life.

INTRODUCTION

What Might Be Happenin' in Heaven

~ Eric ~

*A*ll Heaven was astir! The angelic host had been on the tips of their wings since Sunday night, waiting . . . watching . . . wondering. All the celestial eyes were fixed on the enthusiastic Father who sat on His throne decked out in all His splendor. A myriad of illuminescent seraphs stared at His tender face wondering when His lips would finally utter the much anticipated phrase.

The hours passed, and the expectancy built. It wasn't until Monday night at half past seven that He finally beckoned the archangel to His side. He seemed to giggle as He whispered in Michael's ear. The heavens buzzed with curiosity.

With an exultant smile the King's messenger turned to address the heavenly host. A great "shhhhhhhh!" resounded throughout the inquisitive multitude. Every seraphic and cherubic creature was silent, waiting . . . watching . . . wondering.

The radiant archangel bit his lip attempting not to allow his excitement to overcome him. After a pause that seemed to last a millennium, Michael spoke, his voice peppered with joyful chuckles. "My friends!" His golden voice echoed across the heavens. "The Father says . . . IT'S TIME!!"

Wings fluttered, harps strummed, angelic feet danced on golden streets. It was time! It was *finally* time!!! And all of Heaven was exuberant!

The popcorn vendor arrived just as the big screen began to drop. All the wound-up seraphs found their seats. As the show was starting, the exultant King leaned over and nudged Michael. "I put this one together myself!" He exclaimed.

Michael laughed at the familiar statement and squeezed

the hand of his Hero, the Great Director of Universal Studios.

On the gigantic screen appeared a young man, totally oblivious to the fact that a billion eyes were upon him. It was a rainy night in April. He stood outside the door of a home, waiting . . . watching . . . wondering. In one hand he held a dozen roses, while in the other he clung to a little white box.

The events that would immediately follow had put Heaven on tiptoe. Every angelic being wanted to know how this kid was going to do it. How was he going to surprise her? How would she respond? Would she accept? Only the Almighty Scriptwriter knew, and He was mum on the subject.

The youth fidgeted as the neighbors arrived home and curiously observed him standing there . . . in the rain . . . outside the door of the big blue house.

Suddenly the scene changed. A graceful young lady in a candlelit room came into focus. She was surrounded by her family in what appeared to be a very sentimental moment. Sweet words were spoken, and the little miss was beckoned to sit on a couch with her eyes tightly closed. She was told that they were going outside to get a gift that they had been waiting many years to give her.

The family carefully made their way down the hall, leaving their precious treasure behind. Her eyes squeezed shut in expectation. As they opened the front door to exit, beautiful background music began to play. These were songs that the young lady cherished—songs that caused tears to well within her eyes.

Again the drizzly night and the flower-laden youth appeared on the screen, but this time the door was opening. The young woman's family silently passed through the

doorway and shared a brief moment of tender smiles with the curly-headed young man. Then, quietly, the young man walked through the open doorway.

The door closed behind him. A dark hall, brilliantly lit with nothing but his dreams, greeted him. The stirring melody filled his ears and touched his heart as he tiptoed ever so carefully down the hall. He was but a Cupid's arrow away from the moment he'd anticipated all his life.

Again the rosy-cheeked young maiden came into view. This time it was a close-up of the tears streaming down her soft, delicate face. The music was painting memories of a young man upon her mind. It pained her heart to think that her knight in shining armor was over a thousand miles away. "One day he'll come for me," she assured herself. "He promised he would return."

Unbeknownst to her, the young man stepped into the room. He gazed at her beauty as she gently wept into her hands.

"Leslie!" he whispered with boyish excitement.

The precious princess lifted her head in wonderment. Through a veil of tears she saw an image of her prince. As if it were a dream, she watched him walk toward her and kneel down at her feet. With tears of his own, he sweetly confessed his adoration and love for her. He presented her the blushing roses and the little white box, and with them he also offered his hand.

"My girl, Leslie," his husky voice whispered, "will you marry me?" As he spoke the words, he looked deep into her eyes. The music in the background surged with intensity and great emotion.

Her eyes were wide with ardor, her cheeks flushed with enthusiasm. She was unable to speak. Suddenly the music

climaxed and turned into a flowery melody line. Right at that moment she breathed, "Yes!"

The heavens erupted with emotion. Some angels gave high-fives while others passed around the tissues. "He did it!" a winged-member of the audience bellowed. A chorus of voices broke out in a hip-hop version of "Hallelujah!"

As the big screen rose, the audience moved toward the throne to congratulate the Director. Michael triumphantly winked at the King as the congregation of movie critics surrounded the throne. The King leaned down and whispered in the ear of His beloved archangel. "With as much experience as I have in script-writing, you'd think a few more couples would give Me the opportunity."

Michael smiled at the King and then turned to address the mighty crowd. "I know you are all wondering," he trumpeted, "why it is such a rarity nowadays that we bring the big screen out." He paused and then with great amusement shouted, "There just aren't quality love stories being produced any more that are pure enough to be shown up here!" With that the heavens resounded with laughter. "But," he continued, "it appears as if things are changing down there!"

The celestial throng looked at him with question marks in their eyes. Could it be? Could there be a host of pure love stories just over the horizon?

"Yes, friends," said Michael. "It's true! Our glorious Creator has written the screenplay to thousands of the purest love stories, and He is just waiting for young couples to accept the lead roles!"

The angels looked at each other with joyous anticipation.

Michael continued. "All we need to do is take one very important message to the children down on earth. In fact, this message is so important that the two young people we just

saw in the movie are writing a book about it! Unless the children down on earth understand this message, they will never let the Master Director write their love story. But once they do understand this message, then, my friends, we may well be spending glorious light years watching productions just like the one we saw today!"

"What is the message?!?" the heavenly host asked.

"Simple," replied Michael. "All they really need to know is that the Creator of the Universe . . . LOVES ROMANCE!"

A great cheer arose from the vast host followed by an enormous rustling of wings. Michael finished with one last inspiring challenge: "Let us go to our mission! Let us carry this message to the children on earth. The world will never be the same once they understand *Romance God's Way*!"

And, dear reader, you never can tell how this book may have fallen into your hands. It just might be the mysterious work of an eager messenger of Heaven delivering it straight to you from the Father Himself. Why? Because He may want you to know . . . He's writing a romantic tale *just for you* this very moment!

Chapter 1
That Word!

Eric

I remember the fateful day my mother first uttered *that word*. It stuck in my ear like a prickly in my sock, and it smelled up my cranium like burnt toast does the kitchen. I could never be the same. I mean, how could I after exposure to *that word*?

I had been minding my own business when suddenly my mother's nose began to approach my face like a mad scientist discovering a squashed amoeba under a microscope. I awkwardly pulled away, but the nose persisted—drawing closer . . . and closer . . . and closer. Until finally, "Aha!" My mother had gained the victory. She had discerned the hidden truth. She had discovered . . . peach fuzz! But that wasn't the horrible part. It was the word that followed that lodged a cough drop of awkwardness in my throat.

"Well, Eric, it looks like you are going through . . . " And it was right there she spoke *that word*!

Not much time had passed when again I was exposed to that terrible and hideous word. Again, it was the innocent and unsuspecting mouth of my very own mother from whence it came. This time it was in the kitchen. Little did I know what danger loomed just on the horizon as I staggered, parched and famished, into my favorite room in the house. It was here that I had found refreshment. It was in this very room I had known peace, joy, and satisfaction. But it was here I would come face to face with *that word*!

"Mommy, could I have a glass of milk?" I innocently asked. As I spoke, my voice cracked like a grade AAA egg, and yolk splattered all over my face as I heard my mother giggle.

"Oh, how cute! Eric, you're going through . . . " And there it was, as clear as night, as odiferous as a skunk's behind—*that word!*

Now it's sad to say, but li'l ol' Eric is not the only one who's

been plagued by that one stinkin' word. This word has a reputation! Throughout the centuries, in fact. It has been known to cause hardened criminals to blush. Mothers have experienced tremendous grief, and fathers have gone into hiding due to its simple utterance. And it doesn't just affect common folk. The annals of history reveal that it has defied even the most valiant of knights and menaced even the fairest of princesses. In fact, this crazy word has been known to weaken the knees of the toughest linebacker and turn the heart of the grittiest Navy Seal into Jell-O.

That fateful day in the kitchen was not the last time I would have a head-on collision with *that word*. Pretty soon, pimples began to sprout out of my face like the thistle in our garden, and funny smells began to emerge from my underarms notifying all those up-close and personal that Eric was embarking upon a time in his life called . . . THAT WORD!

Soon all the chaos culminated into one gigantic massacre of my childhood dignity when my dad sat me down for "The Talk." "The Talk" was lacquered with *that word*. Almost every other word was *that word*. Everything that was awkward, everything that was strange, even everything that was greasy, was blamed on *that word*!

One evening my dad had invited me to join him on a drive around town. No particular reason, just an innocent ride around town. It was a conspiracy! I should have smelled it in the air, but my underarms were causing too much of a distraction. We hopped into our banana-yellow VW bus (a beautiful childhood memory) and motored down the street to . . . a parking lot. My dad knew just the right environment to make me comfortable.

Under the auspices of a soccer game strategy session (my dad was my soccer coach and we had a game the following morning), my dad began to talk.

"Soooo, uh, Eric . . . ah, why don't you help me put together the lineups for the game against the Blazers," he mumbled with an awkwardness that filled the banana-yellow bus.

I agreed, and we continued on—staring at a piece of paper my dad had pulled from his briefcase. I could sense a bomb was about to drop.

"Uh, well, why don't we put Luke up here at right wing, and maybe Johnny at left half, and . . . uh . . ." He stopped. Suddenly silence slipped into the bus like a winter chill through a tee shirt. A few seconds passed and then, with the courage of a comic strip exposing itself at the risk of bombing in the Sunday funnies, he spoke.

"Uhhh, yeah, well . . ." He coughed. "Umm . . ." He cleared his throat. "By the way, Eric, there's something I've been meaning to talk to you about." The bomb dropped, and I was the unsuspecting target.

I'll never forget that night in the local parking lot. I spent the entire time staring at the floor of the banana-yellow VW bus with crimson cheeks and ears plugged full of *that word*. In a lifeless monotone, the only thing I said all night was "uh-huh." It was like kissing my brother on the lips and going to school in my underwear all rolled into one! But if *I* thought it was difficult for *me*, just think about my poor dad. He's the one that actually had to speak *that word!*

If I could avoid it, I would never in my entire life even think of *that word* again—let alone hear it, or (gadzooks) ever speak it! But it so happens that a horrible crime has taken place in our society, and the culprit needs to be clearly identified. And yes, that's right—*that word* is a prime suspect! No, this isn't just a trivial charge. This is a capital crime deserving of a punishment that trims the nose hairs to the full extent of the law.

Something in our society has been torturing young minds, plaguing them with insecurity, menacing them with awkwardness. This reprehensible rascal has been known to mislead entire generations of youth from the true beauty of growing up and to dump them in a quandary of funny words and strange misconceptions.

I've taken it upon myself to deal squarely with this scandalous scoundrel and to bring about swift justice. Here, brought forth for your observation, are the most likely suspects, one of which is *that word*.

1) artichokes
2) bedtime
3) homework
4) liver and onions
5) and . . . ah . . . pu . . . pubahh . . . puberty!

Now, it is obvious to us all that each and every one of these poses a tremendous threat to young people, but there is one whose guilt far surpasses all the others. One whose transgressions make these others look like birthday gifts in comparison. Yep! You are absolutely right. It's *that word*! It's *that word* that causes pimples but doesn't tell you how to get rid of them. It's *that word* that transforms you from a cute little kid into a gangly four-eyed greasy-haired nerd without even the politeness to send you a "get-well soon" card. It's *that word* that is solely responsible for confusing us about all those funny things churning inside of us.

I remember looking across the classroom and seeing Cindy McFarlane. *What is THAT?* my mind raced. Another part of me sarcastically answered back, *That's a girl, you idiot!*

Now I knew that Cindy was a girl, but I was sure something had changed. I had been conditioned to respond, "Yuck!" But suddenly, "yuck!" just wasn't capturing what was going on inside of me. Maybe "va-va-voom!!" but not "yuck!"

I was changing! My face was turning fuzzy like a peach, my voice was cracking, and strange other things were taking place that left me looking like a misfit and feeling like a nitwit! I felt like a blob of melting ice cream on the sidewalk. My dad had helped me understand these external changes during "The Talk," but there were a few other things happening as well. Internal things. Desires inside me that I had never known before.

That crazy word, *puberty*, echoed throughout the recesses of my awkwardness and seemed to scream at me: "You good-for-nothing pubertized nerd, just look at yourself in the mirror! Do you think anyone would ever love you when you look like that?"

Never before had I really cared if anyone would ever find me attractive or even if I would ever be lovable. But suddenly that was all I could think about. *Puberty! Puberty! Puberty! You are going through puberty!* That word would ooze into my thoughts. It would pin up pictures of Cindy McFarlane in my brain and then whisper, *Give it up, you brace-faced weirdo!*

Inside me things were taking place that even "The Talk" in the parking lot had not addressed. Suddenly I had a desire to look good. For the past twelve years I didn't care if my hair was standing on end, if my shirt was untucked, if I had pizza sauce dripping down my chin . . . Now, seemingly out of nowhere, I had to look perfect!

Cindy might actually look at me today! I warned myself as I got up an hour earlier than usual to get ready for school.

I began to spend hours picking out just the right outfit; scrubbing my face to try and rid myself of those obscene pimples; and, of course, the most time-consuming item on the morning agenda—styling my hair. I developed a hairdo that was manicured and primped to perfection. It had to be just right. If one hair was out of place, I would skip breakfast to get it exact.

I began to study magazines that had "macho" men in them. I remember browsing through a magazine in which I discovered Arnold Schwarzenegger without a shirt on.

Whoa! So that's what I need to look like? I reasoned.

Immediately I headed to the bathroom and whipped off my shirt. I stared into the mirror with an Eastwood-like smirk and then curled my arms and flexed like I'd seen Arnold do in the magazine. "Bloop!" A tiny little muscle popped out of my arm and then "poof!" I lost it. It was at that moment that I first seriously beheld "The Scrawny One!"

My desire to look good led me to my mother's make-up cabinet one morning before school. My pimples were multiplying like bunny rabbits all over my face, and I couldn't figure out what to do. I found some stuff called "cover-up" in her collection. Stepping in front of the mirror, I carefully dabbed it everywhere I had a blemish.

This was another thing my chat with dad in the banana-yellow VW bus did not cover—makeup. I had absolutely no idea that there are different shades of makeup and that you always need to make sure you match it with your skin color. I mean, how was I supposed to know that?

Well, I learned real quick when sauntering through the boy's locker room that afternoon. One of my "friends" noticed that I had failed to match the appropriate "cover-up" shade with my olive skin. He graciously bellowed, "You're wearing makeup!" I immediately stammered that I surely was not, but he persisted just in case someone had missed his previous declaration. "Eric's wearing makeup!"

Let it suffice it to say that though I desired to look perfect, I was willing to never again wear makeup and to risk having my pimples destroy my image!

Another very pronounced change that was taking place inside of me was the sudden desire to share my life with Cindy McFarlane. It was the strangest thing, but I wanted to know her. And I wanted her to know me! This desire continued to grow . . . and grow . . . and grow.

At first I just would have liked to maybe know her favorite color in the rainbow, but as the weeks and months passed and this desire grew, I would settle for nothing less than to know how her lips would feel pressed up against mine.

I clearly recall watching television when I was younger (that was my first mistake) and seeing a love story unfold

before my very eyes. Boy meets girl. Boy invites girl on date. Boy moves in close. Boy puckers lips. And then boy lays passionate kiss right smack on the girl's ready lips. It seemed so easy, so smooth, so clean. (I never once saw either slobber.) I would sit and stare at this marvel and carefully study how they shaped their lips, how they cocked their heads, and even where they placed their hands.

This kissing stuff was an art, and I had absolutely zero experience. I was confounded as to how those two love-birds even learned to do it. Quickly I became convinced that there was a secret underground kissing school that everyone in the world knew about except for me. Well, if they were not going to invite me, I figured I would have to take the learning into my own hands.

Motionless, I lay in my bedroom, snuggled warmly under my heavy comforter. But, I couldn't sleep. My mind was stuck on Cindy McFarlane! I pictured her lips and attempted to kiss them, but there was no substance. So I reached to my side, grabbed my extra pillow, and drew it close. I puckered my lips and "smackeroo!" my pillow received the kiss I only wished could have landed somewhere on Cindy's adorable face.

Yes, that's right, I confess. *I was a pillow-kisser!* That desire within was growing, and I didn't have a human outlet. Therefore, my pillow became my lone option.

That word—that crazy good-for-nothin' word—had turned me into a four-eyed, brace-faced, greasy-haired, makeup-wearing, Cindy-swooning, pillow-kissing, scrawny Schwarzenegger wanna-be.

It was then I decided that if I was ever going to write a book on the subject of romance, I'd better get my act together and quick.

Chapter 2
Pubertized
and No Way Out!

Eric

*N*early everyone reading this book can identify with something in my last chapter—whether it's *"that word,"* or "The Talk," or "Cindy McFarlane on-the-brain," or maybe even the fact that the only kisses you've ever given have been to your mother, your grandmother, and your pillow. Well, at least now you know there is someone in this world that identifies with your plight! If you ever need a tear of sympathy, just give me a call.

Ahhh! I've been pubertized! Nooooo! Doesn't that sound like some sci-fi movie where a big, fat, ugly monster is eating a poor space cadet alive? For some of us, it's pretty comparable. When we reach eleven, twelve, or thirteen, suddenly this obese, pimply-faced gargoyle named *Puberty* reaches out from underneath our beds in the middle of the night and grabs us. Once it has us, there's no escape!

I don't know if you ever felt this way when you experienced the lovely effects of *that word*, but I sure did. I felt almost like I should be ashamed of what was taking place in my body. I felt bad enough about what was taking place on the outside, but it was the changes on the inside that made me miserable and confused. I wanted to share myself with Cindy McFarlane. I desired a companion in my life. I wanted to love someone, and to be loved in return. And this strange desire didn't just go away with time. It was a *growing* desire.

As the years passed, it kept getting larger . . . and larger . . . and larger. When I reached sixteen, I seriously thought I was going to explode, and there would be little pieces of Eric Ludy splattered all over the walls.

I had this great desire, and I wanted to see it met. But I had one enormous complication. There was one gigantic problem standing between me and a passionate love affair with Cindy McFarlane—GOD! There He was, right in the way! I use to think of Him as the "No-Fun-One." I could

have done whatever I pleased, but the "No-Fun-One" was always right there to shout, "Thou shalt NOT!"

Have you ever thought of God as being a serious-faced, gray-haired guy in the sky whose favorite phrases are: "Aha! Caught ya' red-handed!" and "One more move and I'll strike ya' dead with a bolt of lightning!"?

For some reason, when we're young we have a tendency to associate God with anything that is over-serious and with all those things that are boring and unexciting. "There's NO giggling in God's kingdom, Eric Ludy!" my conscience reprimanded me each time I would start to act up in Junior Sunday School.

I liken it to the "nutrition principle." If I were to mention all sorts of scrumptious foods like brownies, ice cream, and sugar cereals, what could you instantly tell me about their nutritional value? Yep, you're right! Since they taste good, we can automatically assume that they are bad for us. Yet what if I mentioned some rather bland and dull foods like broccoli, cauliflower, and bean sprouts? What could you tell me about their nutritional value? Yep, you're right again! Because they are boring and tasteless, we can safely assume that they must be good for us.

The "nutrition principle" simply states that what is delicious and enjoyable is bad for us, and what is bland and boring is good for us.

During those pubertized years, we are suddenly struck with the possible thrill of enjoying the opposite sex. BUT— we can just feel God breathing over our shoulder saying, "Have you read Leviticus lately?" God and our sexuality are like oil and water—they don't mix. Why? Because God is dull, and anything associated with the area of our sexuality is thrilling.

We can imagine God creating mankind. We can see Him shaping the head, molding the arms and legs, and we can even imagine Him carving out the belly button. But *never, EVER* could we imagine Him to be the proud inventor of those (ahem) parts—you know (cough), in the middle of our bodies. It's almost as if we picture God slipping up when He was creating Adam. And when He said it was "very good," He hadn't yet realized His mistake. When He did discover His error, He just slapped a fig leaf over it!

How far from the Truth this thinking is! When we are pubertized, it's strictly God's doing! He's the creator of puberty. Well maybe I should say He's the creator of that season of our lives. I can't imagine God using *that word* to describe anything! Nevertheless, all those crazy things that are taking place within our bodies during that time are a result of His brilliance and ingenuity. Most shocking of all, though, is the news about that growing desire we have erupting within us to share our lives with someone of the opposite sex. God even put *that* there! Purposely, and I'm not joking!

God doesn't view "the puberty years" of your life as a time of brace-faced awkwardness. He sees it completely different than that. In fact, if God were to have a title for this season of our lives, it would surely be something beautiful and ennobling. You see, guys, God wants us to understand that in this season of our lives He is molding us into men and hewning us into hunks. Ladies, this is the time of your life that you are being transformed into a princess and changed into a fragrant rose.

Doesn't that sound romantic? Just as a farmer plants in the spring so that he can reap a harvest in the fall, God

plants the seeds of manhood and womanhood in us (respectively) during this season so that we may bear the fruit of mature adulthood as the years pass.

If any of you are wondering when we're going to start talking about romance, the time has come! All of this talk about *that word* was to bring us to the understanding that what has taken place inside us is a miraculous work of God. Including that growing desire for companionship that begins to stir, and knock, and bang as the years come and go. Most of us have never realized that God has placed within us that desire to love and be loved. Therefore, we don't seek after Him to discover what He wants us to do with it.

Believe it or not, God has a way of dealing with this growing desire. It is a way that maybe you've never before thought of—a way that, contrary to the "nutrition principle," is full of amazing beauty, indescribable joy, and matchless romance. It is a way that the enemy has worked overtime to keep us away from because when we discover it, the destiny God has for our lives unfolds before us.

As Leslie and I share it with you, you'll find it to be shockingly simple yet profoundly challenging. You'll discover why the enemy has tried so hard to confuse us and to lead us away from *Romance God's Way*. God's version of romance makes the world's version look like a candlelit dinner on a garbage dump! *Romance God's Way* is far more challenging, yet a million times more fulfilling!

Most people think that God's way of going about finding a marriage partner is: The World's Way *plus* a whole list of "thou shalt not's." But God's way cannot even be compared to the way the world has trained and

conditioned us to discover love. It is completely different and beautifully unique.

This will be more than just a journey to discover a better approach to romance. Hopefully it will be an encounter with the person of God! Since God is the inventor of romance, we can't sidestep Him in our pursuit of its purpose. He knows better than any of us why He placed that intrinsic magnet within us that draws us to the opposite sex.

Before you read any further, I challenge you to ask yourself this question: *Am I willing to be changed by God?* You see, if you are willing, God is ready and willing to do the work. Allow Him to correct your pubertized thinking. Allow Him to show you His true nature. And most of all allow Him to take a hold of your life and shape you into His very likeness.

The first and greatest question we must start with is: *What is the difference between the world's way and God's way?*

Chapter 3
Learning the World's Way ...the Hard Way

Leslie

I'll never forget the moment I first saw *him*. He glanced my way from across the room, and his cobalt blue eyes grabbed my attention. His handsome features and sandy blonde hair were irresistible. He was tall (about 5 feet 2 inches) athletic, popular . . . everything I could hope for. Yes, from that moment on I knew I had found the man of my dreams!

Of course, when you're a thirteen-year-old girl in Mrs. Johnson's eighth grade computer class, you see the world through eyes that think they know everything there is to know about love and romance. I mean, the guy is gorgeous and popular! What more is there?

For almost thirteen long years—well, okay, maybe more like three or so, I had been waiting for the time when I would begin that wonderful, life-changing experience called "dating." Now I was chomping at the bit, ready to hit the scene. On that memorable day when I first laid eyes on him, I knew I couldn't wait any longer. I just *had* to have a boyfriend, and it *had* to be him!

For several weeks I "drooled" over Johnny [that's not his real name]. Computer class was suddenly my favorite subject. I doubt if I learned more than how to start my computer, but I spent plenty of time studying Johnny's eyes, smile, and personality. I wondered if he would ever talk to me. I'd seen him looking my way more than a few times, always flashing me one of his thrilling smiles, but we'd never once come close enough to actually have a conversation.

My lucky day finally came when Mrs. Johnson assigned us to be lab partners. Johnny seemed just as pleased about it as I was, and soon we were chatting and laughing together like old friends. He had a personality to match his looks. I couldn't wait to be with him each day.

"What's going on between you and Johnny?" my friends would ask me in the halls.

I'd giggle and tell them all about what he said to me or how he smiled at me five times in one hour! "That's got to mean something, don't you think?" I'd ask them with a confident smile.

"He'll ask you out by the end of the week, definitely!" they would assure me.

I was quickly gaining attention and popularity from my "friendship" with Johnny, and I was really enjoying it!

Finally the day came when he "asked me out" via one of his sidekick friends. I was electrified! I hardly knew what to say.

I must interject for those who have not recently experienced the eighth grade melodrama, "going out" does not mean a guy asks you on a date (most of us were not allowed to officially "date"), but rather he is asking you to be "his girlfriend." That means holding hands in the hall, writing notes to each other, talking together for hours on the phone, and making sure all your friends refer to you as a couple. As a thirteen-year-old, "going out" with someone (especially someone like Johnny!) suddenly graduates you from "little kid" to "mature-adult-in-a-serious-relationship."

We thought we were quite sophisticated! All of us lived in our own little eighth grade soap opera, and every "relationship" was what our little world was built around. So when Johnny asked me out, I had finally arrived into this world. I was loving every minute of it!

Going out with the "man of my dreams" was great at first. I might have been a bit of a space-case in the eighth grade, but I had good solid morals. And not only was Johnny handsome and popular, he had good solid morals

too. Some of my peers were already sleeping around with guys and changing boyfriends as often as they changed clothes. Yes, I know we are talking about thirteen and fourteen-year-olds, but it's the sad truth! They were beginning to experiment with drugs and drinking, and many of them had terrible grades in school. I had been raised in a Christian home and knew right from wrong, so I tried to avoid friendships with this crowd.

The friends I hung out with were prone to lying, cheating, gossiping, and bad language, but they weren't *really* bad. This eased my conscience. And even though Johnny was good-looking and popular, he didn't pressure me to have sex with him. I was sure I had found the best of both worlds.

Johnny and I were a "couple" for the rest of the school year. We began spending more and more time together. Each night we would talk on the phone for at least an hour or two. He was meeting a need within me to be found attractive and to be loved. Sure, I was confident that my parents loved me, but this was totally different. This was actually an attractive, popular member of the opposite sex choosing to be in a relationship with *me*! I'd share my thoughts, dreams, and emotions with him, and he would listen and understand. His praise and flattery kept me going through a time that would otherwise have been lonely and insecure.

"I love you" he would tell me passionately every day. I'll admit that at first I did feel a little strange accepting "love" from a guy who was fourteen years old and who had only been tall enough to ride the roller coaster at Six Flags for less than a year, but I figured that was just something that all couples said to each other. After a few months of hearing it, however, I started to believe him. Soon I was addicted to hearing those words.

Because by this time we were so emotionally hooked on one another, we began to need to express our "love" in deeper ways than just words. I had made a commitment to abstinence until marriage and I had no intention of breaking that, but I'm sorry to admit that Johnny and I began to do things physically that I never thought I would be tempted to do.

Every time I heard him say "I love you," and every time I shared a piece of my heart with him, my resolve weakened in the area of our physical relationship. I was just so dependent upon his affection. We never went "all the way" physically, but we did so much more than was wise. And each time we touched, a deeper part of me was given to him.

Looking back, I cringe to think of that time. How could I have given something so sacred to a fourteen-year-old kid who only wanted to feed his own needs and desires? What a waste! We might have thought of ourselves as "mature adults in a serious relationship," but in reality we had no idea that what we were doing was going to affect us for the rest of our lives.

Our relationship continued for about ten months. My friends all admired our "commitment" to each other and marveled at how long we'd been together. Having Johnny in my life brought me such security, I never considered breaking up with him. Just simply having a boyfriend made me feel worth something. But as we graduated from middle school to high school, I began to realize that this was the time in my life to hit the "dating scene." There were plenty of other guys around, and I began to wonder what it would be like to start dating someone else. Finally, we both realized it was time to move on.

I didn't think it would be hard to break up with Johnny. After all, I had never really been "serious" about him—I mean, I never planned on getting married to him or anything. Now

that I was in high school, there were at least a hundred other guys I could go out with that were just as good-looking and nice as Johnny. But it wasn't that simple. The night we officially ended our relationship over the phone, a shock wave ran throughout my emotions. We may as well have called it a divorce! I simply wasn't expecting the inner turmoil "breaking up" caused.

"My life is over!" I sobbed hysterically, throwing myself across my bed. I cried until I had no more tears.

I was an emotional wreck. For days I couldn't eat or sleep. I was desperately confused and hurt. I couldn't understand why this experience was so traumatic for me.

Looking back, I see now what I didn't see then. For months I had been emotionally secure in my relationship with "my eighth grade dream-boat." Although I hadn't completely given myself away to him physically, emotionally I had entirely offered myself to him without even realizing it. I had relied on him for my security and comfort, and for ten months he had soothed the aching need within me to be loved and cherished by someone of the opposite sex. How did I expect to end something like that without someone getting hurt? Like I mentioned earlier, I was a little bit of a flake back then!

After my "relationship" with Johnny ended, I was so desperate for "guy attention" that I started entering one relationship after another. Each time, I came out heartbroken. But I kept on dating, and I kept on getting my emotions crushed and stepped on. My heart had become so worthless—I would just give it away, let it get broken, pick up the pieces, and do it all over again. There was no other

alternative. (Other than not dating at all, which was about as out of the question as you could get.)

I had looked forward for so long to finally being able to be a part of the dating scene. It was going to be so much fun and so romantic. I kept telling myself that one of these days I would start really enjoying it. But for some reason that day never came. Where was the fun? Where was the romance? What had I done wrong? By the age of fifteen, I felt as if I had been married and divorced three or four times. My heart was nothing more than hamburger meat now.

It was in this state of hopelessness that God began to speak to my heart. One day I was reading my Bible—something I had begun to do less and less of since I had hit the dating scene. A verse in Proverbs 31 caught my attention. You know, the chapter that describes "a wife of noble character"?

Now, just to make this clear, I didn't often sit around and read verses about marriage. Marriage seemed WAY down the road, and I was not going to worry about that for a long time. But this verse was speaking about a godly wife. It said, "She does him good and not evil all the days of her life."

Wait a minute! *All* the days of her life? You mean she's thinking about her husband before she even meets him? How would she be able to "do him good" all the days of her life, when she doesn't even know where he is or what he's doing?

I thought about my future husband. I supposed he was out there . . . somewhere. Was I doing him good? I had always assumed I was doing all I could do for him in not having sex before marriage. I mean, that was way more

than most everyone else was doing! But then it occurred to me that I had more than just a physical treasure to save for him . . . One day I would give him the treasure of my heart and my emotions. I certainly hadn't done a very great job in saving *that* treasure.

My emotions were being beaten and battered with every relationship I entered into. When I was younger, I used to think that by the time I was ready to get married, I would have forgotten all about the other guys I dated in high school and college. Anyone who has ever been in a relationship knows that is impossible. You can't forget. Every person you give your emotions to is etched deeply upon your heart and memory.

Foamy or Firm?

Imagine that I came up to you one day and offered you a very valuable diamond. (I know that the girls might get a little more excited than the guys over this; but guys, just think, if you're not into diamond rings, you can always trade it in and use the money for a car!) The only catch about this gift is that you can't use the diamond in any way for five years. You need to carefully watch over it until that time comes.

You now have a small problem. You have a very valuable treasure, and you need a place to keep it for the next five years where it will be safe. So, you ask me if I have any ideas.

Well, I have two options for you. The first is a Styrofoam cup. It has many advantages including the fact that it's absolutely FREE! On your student budget, that's always good. And it's especially easy to take care of—I mean, you don't even need to wash it, shine it, or polish it! When you are done using it, you simply throw it away!

Have I convinced you yet? The Styrofoam cup is an excellent container, right? What's that? You say you want to look at the negative side? Okay. Well, this cup does have a few *small* disadvantages when you're trying to store something valuable inside it. For instance, you never know who might get a hold of one of these cups. Like your neighbor's dog for instance.

Dogs have a strange attraction to these cups. They have even been known to chew them up and spit them back out. Now, if your diamond just happened to be in one of these cups at the time your neighbor's dog decided to have a feast, well . . . bye, bye diamond. Soon your treasure would be in the belly of your neighbor's dog, and I seriously doubt the humane society would let you perform surgery on the dog to get your treasure back. You'd only have one choice. Do what one lady in Denver had to do when her dog ate her diamond ring. Give him ipecac syrup and make him throw up about seven times. Then put some rubber gloves on and go through the nasty stuff to retrieve your diamond. What? Lost your appetite? Oh, sorry. So, maybe the cup isn't the best option for your diamond, huh?

Styrofoam cups also can easily get squished or thrown away by accident, so you're probably right—Styrofoam isn't the greatest material to use for storing a valuable treasure. It simply isn't made to last! Styrofoam cups are really only designed to be used for a picnic or barbecue and then tossed in the trash. But the point is, you don't want Styrofoam for your diamond.

Okay, here's option two. I have a solid silver mug that Eric's mom recently gave me. It's a very special family heirloom because it has E-R-I-C engraved across the front of it. It was his baby cup, and his parents had it engraved. It's been around for twenty-five years. I've never once seen

a dog try to chew it up, nor has anyone tried to throw it away. So, yes, it would be a much safer place for your diamond.

Does this option have disadvantages? A few. First of all, it's going to cost you. Big time! I mean, I'm not just going to *give* you a family heirloom, am I? Especially since it has E-R-I-C engraved on the front of it! This is worth a lot, so you'll probably have to get a summer job just to cover the cost of buying it from us.

The other negative is that caring for it takes a little more work. You have to clean it, polish it, and maybe even dust it. It's not quite as easy to care for as the Styrofoam cup. But at the end of five years, you are sure to have your diamond intact. No dog in his right mind will try to chew up a silver mug. (Even a dog *not* in his right mind probably wouldn't try it!) And I doubt anyone will throw it away. Your diamond is safe in this silver mug, and you know that in five years you'll reap the benefits of making this decision.

How many of you, when given these two options, would actually be crazy enough to stick your valuable diamond into a little Styrofoam cup? Hopefully, none of you!

Well, think about this. Your emotions are a treasure, a gift from God. Your heart is so much more valuable than any diamond. Someday you will give that treasure to your future spouse. Are you taking good care of it? Or is your diamond in a Styrofoam cup right now, getting chewed up, stepped on, and thrown away?

I remember my first day of fifth grade. My friends and I piled into the classroom joking and giggling. When our teacher walked into the room, we had one thing on our minds . . . how far was he going to let us push him? Was

he going to be an easy teacher? Just how much were we going to be able to get away with this year?

"In my class, you can do anything you want." Those were the first words out of his mouth. We looked at each other excitedly, hardly daring to believe our good fortune.

This is great, we were thinking. *Let's party! We can draw faces on the chalkboard, smush crayons into the carpet, doodle on our homework paper . . ."*

"You can do anything you want in my class," he said again, "as long as you are willing to face the consequences of your actions."

Whoa! *Consequences?* That was a heavy word! We all changed our attitude real fast. We sat up straight, looked at the teacher, refrained from giggling and talking, and always turned in our homework paper with *no doodles!* Why? Simple. Consequences! We realized from our teacher's statement that we were either going to be punished or rewarded for the decisions we made in class each day. Of course, that was back in the days when school principals were still allowed to use wooden paddles! Just one fleeting thought of being sentenced to an interview with "Mr. Paddle" was enough to make us get our act together.

Consequences were one thing I just didn't understand when I was in that relationship with Johnny, or in any of the relationships I had. I didn't realize that each choice I made would affect my future marriage in either a positive or negative way.

Sure, I knew that having sex before marriage would somehow hurt my future relationship, but beyond that, I didn't see how a few casual dating relationships could possibly do me any harm. I looked at my high school and college years as one big party—have fun now, be serious later. I was just

going to date around "for fun" for a few years, then someday, way down the road, I would meet "Mr. Right." We'd fall in love, get married, and live happily ever after.

Sounds easy enough, doesn't it? Unfortunately, I didn't have a clue about the way things really are—that is, until God began to challenge me to start thinking about my future husband.

I finally realized that my heart was a treasure that I should have been carefully guarding and protecting for him. I was giving that treasure to one guy and then another. Each time it was becoming less and less beautiful and pure. My future marriage suddenly became something I wanted to work for, to invest in, to make beautiful and strong. And for the first time, I discovered how to live that way even before I met the man I'd be spending my life with.

Temporary dating relationships—giving and receiving emotions and affections for the sake of short-lived security or pleasure—were doing nothing to build up my future marriage relationship. They were only tearing it down. My diamond was becoming less and less attractive! I saw that no matter how much I desired to date around and experience some incredible "teen romance," even more I wanted to invest into the one relationship that was going to last for a lifetime . . . my future marriage.

"Okay, Lord, whatever it takes, I'll do it. Just show me how to invest in my future marriage and to love my future husband. I'm tired of giving my heart away to one guy and then another. Show me what you want me to do, Lord. I'm willing."

Dun, dun, dun dun, dunnnnn . . . Dark, foreboding music played in the back of my mind as soon as I uttered this prayer. *What have I done? What is God going to ask me to do now? Oh no, if HE gets a hold of this area of my*

life, He'll ruin me!!!

Fear gripped me as I realized what I had just said to God, because as soon as I said those words, I knew what He was asking me to do . . . Give up the dating scene! Ahhhh!! NO!!! How can I possibly do that? That's ridiculous! That's insane!

"Listen, God, You don't really understand my predicament here, so let me explain. I'm sixteen years old. Now I know in Heaven that may not mean much, but down here on earth, sixteen is *the* age to live! Life revolves around parties and dances and . . . DATING! If I give that up, I'll be a nobody! So, you see, God, I really can't help you out on this one, but thanks for asking! I know You meant well."

As much as I wanted to take back my "Lord, I am willing" prayer, I couldn't. I knew what God was asking me to do, and as much as I hated to admit it, I knew He was right. I couldn't be a part of the dating scene anymore if I truly wanted to follow His will and invest in my relationship with my future husband.

So on that fateful day in February, at sixteen years old, I officially gave up dating. My commitment was to simply dedicate myself fully to serving God and to trust that in His time, in His way, He would bring my future husband into my life. Until then, I wasn't even going to look for him. I was going to trust God, wait patiently, and set myself apart—physically and emotionally—for this man I would one day marry.

It was a valiant and courageous decision . . . but I was not at all valiant or courageous about making it! Awful visions filled my head of what would become of me. I pictured a young dismal teenager, sitting in a rocking chair

and staring out the window every night of the week. No phone calls. No friends. No life. Just rocking, rocking, rocking. I just *knew* I had signed my life away.

Some of my friends heard about my decision and rolled their eyes in disgust. "How do you ever expect to get married, Leslie, if you're not dating? How do you expect some Prince Charming to just come knock on your door if he doesn't even know you exist! You are being so stupid!"

Great! Thanks for the encouragement. Just what I needed to hear, girls!

What I didn't yet perceive were the *awesome* plans God had in store for me . . . just around the corner! All He needed was for me to take that one first step of obedience and say, "Lord, I am willing." A beautiful love story was about to be written. And this may surprise you, but it started the very day I made my commitment to stop dating!

How? Simple! My love for my future husband had to start first with my love for Jesus Christ. No marriage can last unless it's built on the love of Jesus instead of human love. So when I decided to lay down dating relationships and focus on Jesus, I took the first step toward building a strong love relationship with my future husband.

Jesus once said, "You cannot serve both God and money." The same is true with dating relationships. *You cannot serve both God and dating.*

Dating relationships had become the focus of my life even though I never would have admitted it. If someone had asked me, I would have said, "God is number one in my life." Yet was it God that I spent hours and hours talking with each day? Was it God that consumed every thought? Was it God that I spent endless nights daydreaming about? Was it God that my friends and I constantly talked about?

Did I hang posters of God on my bedroom wall? No! It was GUYS! Guys were a constant distraction to me. I would spend all my time and energy trying to flirt with them, look right for them, impress them. I had very little time left over for God.

Well, after my "Lord, I am willing" prayer, things changed. Jesus Christ became real to me! I began to realize that I had been gradually pushing Him out of my life to do my own thing. Now, I wanted to get to know Him again.

Instead of spending my spare time focused on guys, I started focusing on Him. I started a journal, and each day I wrote to God about my fears, dreams, and desires. I spent hours studying the Bible and looking for ways to apply it to my life. I really began to fall in love with Jesus! He began to be so near, so real.

After a few months of my new commitment to "not date," I suddenly realized that *He* was meeting all my needs. I didn't *need* a boyfriend to be happy! I didn't *need* to be in the dating scene to be happy! I was finally content in my relationship with Jesus Christ.

This was the first step I took toward loving my future husband. Good strong marriages MUST be built on the principle of loving Jesus Christ first—finding contentment in Him alone. And though that time wasn't easy, as the weeks passed, I knew that God had something very special on the horizon.

Now flee from youthful lusts,
and pursue righteousness, faith, love and peace,
with those who call on the Lord from a pure heart.
2 Timothy 2:22 NASB

Lord, I see how I have been living selfishly in this area of my life. I have bought into the world's system which has told me to do things my own way. I have been giving away my heart and emotions, and I haven't been saving myself for that one special person You have chosen for me. I ask Your forgiveness. I now choose, from this day on, to live to honor and love my future spouse—to keep myself pure both physically and emotionally for the one I will spend my life with. I choose to back away from temporary relationships and trust that You will bring that person to me in Your own perfect timing. Until that time, help me make You my number one focus.

Lord, I Am Willing
Leslie Ludy

I've said it many times before,
But Lord, I want this time to be . . .
Knowing with my heart, believing with my soul,
I am willing to give You all of me.

I place my life into Your hands
And say, "Do with me what You will."
No matter where You take me, Lord,
If I have You, I am fulfilled.

Lord, I am willing
To do what You want me to do.
Lord, I am willing
To surrender all I am to You.
Wherever You take me,
Whatever I become,
Lord, I am willing, in my life
Your will be done.

Chapter 4
Card House or Castle?

Eric

*W*hen I was a pimply-faced thirteen-year-old and felt bored, I had a special place where I would go and let my imagination run free. I'd burrow into my dirty closet and clear a place on the floor where I could empty my treasure chest. Now, girls, remember—a guy's treasure is often different than a lady's!

I would take the cardboard top off my faded red shoebox and remove my priceless gems. Oh so carefully I would extrapolate the rubber band from the pile of jewels and one by one intoxicate myself with their splendorous beauty. Okay, okay—maybe my collection of baseball cards was a little dinged up. Maybe they had scribbles on them. Maybe some of them even had marks of my younger brother's thoughtfulness and love (he once threw up on my collection in the middle of the night mistaking the box for the trash can), but these cards were my treasure.

I would spend hours lying on the floor of my closet staring at them. I'd memorize the players' heights, weights, dates-of-birth, and, of course, all their lifetime statistics. And I'd imagine myself in their spikes, rounding the bases after a grand slam—maybe even one day having my beefy body (I weighed around 89 lbs. and that's being generous) on a baseball card too.

Believe it or not, even sorting through all my thousands of cards would eventually get dull. To avoid the undesirable affects of the "summer-time blues," I was motivated to concoct a Plan B. "B" standing for Build.

With the hands of a surgeon, I would very deftly and gingerly stand up two cards against each other, carefully place one on top of them, and slowly but surely build a magnificent card house. But it didn't take me long to learn that all it took was one wrong move and *whoosh*, my card house went *kapooie*. The dinkiest error, the most minute

slip, the slightest breeze, and it was over!

Usually that slight breeze was very graciously offered by my younger brother. Leave it to Marky to come roaring into the room without even a hint of a knock. Almost like clockwork, as that all-important card was delicately being placed at the most crucial spot of my amazing superstructure, the door would burst open. My card house would be history, and usually my mouth would be washed out with soap by my mother for my verbal retaliation.

As trying as those times were, with every failure I faced in erecting a house of cards, God was planting seeds of truth inside my mind and heart.

My frustration led me to the doorstep of Card Houses Unlimited, a customer service corporation somewhere in my wild imagination. Ready to voice my complaint, I raised my hand to pound on the door. Suddenly my eye caught a note nailed to their doorpost. It contained this rudimentary principle of card houses:

> *Hey, Turkey! What did you expect?*
> *They are built for laughs, not to last!*

Sentimental tears flowed from my eyes as I walked away pondering that heart-wrenching message. Never again would I entertain the thought, *My children sure will enjoy this card house someday.* I had to swallow the fact that they would never see it. Gulp!

Well, I had another favorite pastime that offered similar challenges and identical lessons. I was raised as a Ludy to salivate at the sight of a sandy beach. Ludy motto: *Where there is beach, we must build!*

Beach was synonymous with "sand castle" where I grew up. My dad was famous throughout our entire family reunion

for his uncanny artistic flare in the medium of wet sand. And I'm proud to say, the expertise was passed on—okay, okay, to my brother, but the point is, it was passed on!

We would spend an entire Saturday afternoon carefully hollowing out moats, creatively shaping towers, masterfully crafting castle walls, when suddenly . . . the tide would turn! In but a few minutes, all we had to show for an entire day's work was the blurry Polaroid snapshot taken by li'l cousin Joey on accident. The entire day's work was totally washed away! Nothing was even left to prove all our hours of hard labor to the women when they returned from shopping.

As my frustration escalated over the years, I was forced to visit the doorstep of Sand Castles International, another very helpful customer service corporation. Nailed to their doorpost, I spotted a sign similar to the one I had read before. It said:

> *Hey, Turkey! Haven't I seen you before?*
> *Read my lips:*
> *If it's built in one afternoon,*
> *it's sure to come to ruin.*
> *What is meant to last,*
> *must not be built too fast!*

My over-pubertized brain was struggling to grasp this simple concept, but finally it began to sink in. *You mean, even though I spend an entire afternoon constructing a masterpiece, I'll never be able to show it off to my wife someday?* my mind would reason.

Slowly I was coming to the realization that card houses and sand castles have one enormous thing in common: Neither is built to last! When the slightest change in environment comes (i.e. the wind blows or the tide turns), the

houses collapse even quicker than the time it took to build them. They don't last because they have not been built upon a solid foundation.

Jesus gives us a profound parable in the book of Matthew, chapter seven. He introduces us to two men—an idiot and a wise man.

The idiot I find to be a lot like me during my weaker moments. He's looking for the easy way to accomplish his task. He's the ultimate cheapskate who's always in a rush and who never listened to his mother when she told him, "Patience is a virtue!" He builds a house, but he builds it on the sand. Jesus says, and I paraphrase, "What an idiot!"

You see, the idiot may have his house, but he did not build with a future in mind. In other words, he didn't consider the fact that wind and rain *will* eventually come. He never pondered the ominous fact that seasons change and tides *do* turn. And when they do, it doesn't take a biophysicist to figure out what happens. *Kapooie!* And all the idiot had to show for his work were scrapes, slivers, and a horrible headache. (Just imagine a house falling on you!)

Now, before you get teary-eyed, let me remind you that there was another builder. Who? *The WISE builder!* It's not that he even did anything extraordinary, he simply built his house right. He thought, *If I'm going to build a house that will last, I think I should probably start by laying a foundation.* Let's all applaud this man's awe-inspiring ingenuity and extraordinary insight.

The wise man simply realized that to face the challenges the future *would* hold, he must solidly undergird his home. What this man chose to do, hopefully, is no different than what we would do if we were preparing to build a house. You see, a foundation is the key to stability

and the secret to a house's longevity. The broader and deeper the foundation, the higher you can build. And the more solid your foundation, the tougher it is for the house to fall.

Have you ever considered that relationships with the opposite sex are built much like a house is built? Just like a house without a foundation, a relationship built without a future in mind will crumble to the ground at the first sight of storm clouds.

Ironically, just like the idiot and the wise builder, there are two types of relationship developers: the stupid and the smart.

The stupid—not realizing, of course, that he is stupid—goes about building a relationship quickly. He only thinks about what he can gain for the least amount of expenditure. He doesn't consider the fact that when the relational storms of life come, he has nothing to hold his love shack together.

"Now who," you ask, "would be so brazenly stupid to build a relationship like that?" Well, I for one built quite a few relationships like that in my younger, more idiotic days. I was building relationships that couldn't have lasted even if I had wanted them to. I sure wasn't preparing myself for marriage which is intended to last a lifetime.

God wanted to teach me how to be a *smart* builder. And he didn't just want me to build myself a house—He wanted to teach me how to build a castle of dreams! A relationship that's not just satisfactory, but sensational!

Now, I had experience in building card houses, but I had no idea what I was getting into when God started showing me the floor plan for a castle. First, I had to brush

up on my history and learn some things about castles.

A castle was another term for fort or buttress. Castles were huge structures built in ancient times that could house an entire city when an army invaded the land. They stood out like a Roman nose and were noticeably different than the cottages that speckled the countryside—not only in structure and size, but in beauty and grace.

The nobility lived in castles, and if you were a prince or princess, you were bound to have a castle for your home. But there was one important thing we must note: *Castles took years to build!* You see, castles were built to last thousands of years. Because of that, they not only demanded forethought, they also cost the builder a great deal. They demanded the commitment of the builder, but the builder always knew that the end result would far outweigh the temporary sacrifices.

God wants us to build our future marriage relationship like we were building a castle. Why? Because marriages and castles are both intended to be built to last.

If you travel around Europe today, you will see castles built hundreds, even thousands, of years ago, dressing the landscape. That's what God desires our marriages to be like—a testimony to the generations to come of how a relationship can brave the storms of life when it is built right. But just like the wise builder, we must first lay a proper foundation.

How many of you, when you visit a beautiful home, make mention to the owner of how lovely its foundation is?

Ridiculous, right? We never notice the foundation of a house. It's not the attractive element of a house, but it's the necessary one. You could have all the crystal chandeliers in the world, but if you did not have a solid foundation, your house would fall flat.

Foundation-laying is not the fun part; concrete pouring never is. The color gray is not too appealing to the eye, and it's certainly not very romantic. But unless that foundation is properly laid, there is no reason to even waste your time with all the "fun" stuff.

So get on your grubbies! We'll supply the shovel, and let's dig deep into our hearts and get ready for the hard work of romance.

Throughout the remainder of this book we will be talking about how to build a castle of dreams. As we explore the first and most important step, just remember that the foundation stone of a lifelong relationship doesn't have anything directly to do with your future spouse, but everything to do with your relationship with Jesus Christ.

"Everyone who hears these words of Mine,
and acts upon them,
may be compared to a wise man,
who built his house upon the rock."
Matthew 7:24 NASB

Lord, help me lay a strong foundation for my future relationship with my spouse. I want a marriage that will stand the test of time. Give me the strength and courage to build a foundation Your way.

Your Castle of Dreams

By now you've probably decided to start building a castle instead of a card house. If so, congratulations! This process is long and difficult, but you'll never regret the hard work once you receive the reward it brings.

STEP 1 on the work list: pouring the cement. Translated into relationships that means—

surrendering to God and learning to trust Him.

Chapter 5
Bread in the Barnyard?

Leslie

*W*hen I was six years old, one of my favorite pastimes was listening to my little red and white plastic Mattel record player which played 45 RPM records of nursery stories. There were little picture books that you could look at as the record played, and whenever it was time to turn the page, the record would screech with a high pitched "Dinnnng!"

One of my favorites was the story of the Little Red Hen. It was such a wonderful story, that I would like to share it with all of you right now. Aren't you excited? Well, okay, here we go.

The Little Red Hen was in the barnyard one day, and she decided to bake a loaf of bread. (Please don't ask me why in the world a hen in a barnyard wants to make bread. That's entirely beside the point here!) So she went to the horse and asked, "Will you help me gather the wheat?"

The horse said, "No, I can't help you gather the wheat. I am much too busy!" (And please don't ask me what in the world a horse could be busy doing while standing around in a barnyard because I have no idea, but I guess that's the horse's business and not ours.)

So the Little Red Hen went to the pig and repeated her question.

"No, I am much too busy to help you gather the wheat," replied the pig. (Okay, so these are barnyard animals with a *social life*! What can I say?)

So the Little Red Hen went to all the other barnyard animals to ask if they could help her gather the wheat. To spare you the grief of going through each barnyard animal, I will simply tell you that they ALL said the same thing. They were too busy to help her gather the wheat. So the Little Red Hen had to gather the wheat all by herself.

"Dinnnng!" (Time to turn the page of the picture book.)

Then the Little Red Hen needed to grind the wheat. So, of course, she went to all the animals, and, of course, they were still all to busy to help her. (The barnyard was a really happenin' place, as I'm sure you've realized by now.) So she ground the wheat alone.

Then it was time to mix the dough. Same situation. All too busy.

"Dinnng!" (Time to turn the page again.)

(In case you haven't noticed, I am really breezing through this story, and I'm leaving out a lot of important details. If you really want the full effect, you'd better go buy the Mattel record player!)

So the same thing happened when she needed to bake the bread. Everyone was too busy to help. Poor Little Red Hen. Don't you start to feel for her after awhile? I bet you're thinking to yourself, *I would help the Little Red Hen!* Well, of course, you would! So would I! But these barnyard animals are just pitiful excuses for neighbors, and you can't really blame them. I mean, look at the neighborhood they come from!

Anyway, it came time for the Little Red Hen to take the bread out of the oven. The smell of fresh baked goods filled the barnyard (nicely overpowering some of the *other* smells that were lingering in the air). Little Red Hen asked who would like to help her *eat* the bread.

"I will!" said all of the barnyard animals in unison. They rushed forward, eager to devour the treat. But the Little Red Hen was one smart chick. (No pun intended!) She told them, "NO! You were all too busy to help me gather the wheat, grind the wheat, mix the dough, and

bake the bread, so you don't deserve to eat the bread! I will eat it myself!" And she did!

Great story, right? Yes, *I* thought so. Now, okay, I know you are sitting there right now thinking, *Where in the world is Leslie going with this?* Hey, relax! I DO have a point. Just keep reading . . .

Every young person we've talked to about the area of relationships with the opposite sex has the same desire—to have a relationship that is beautiful and lasting. No one (at least no one in his or her right mind) has great ambitions to grow up, get married, and get divorced. That isn't usually at the top of anyone's list of lifelong goals! You are probably no different. You desire to have a great love life and find a relationship that will stand the test of time. But here's a key question . . . Are you willing to do whatever it takes to see that happen? Even if it means something like (gasp) *surrendering* this area to Jesus Christ?! Ouch! That hurts.

Do we trust Him, or do we trust ourselves more? For a while, I had been so sure I didn't need God's help in this area of my life. I knew what I was looking for in a man and I figured He didn't. But strangely, all my confidence got me nowhere in the area of relationships. When I did it my way, I ended up with a broken heart every time. Finally, I came to the conclusion that since God created me, He knew every dream and desire of my heart. He knew what was in store for my future. So after days of struggling, crying, and doubting, I *finally* came to the place where I was ready to surrender this part of my life to His Lordship. Only then was He free to paint a beautiful love story in my life . . . *His way*.

"I want to have a love story *just* like yours and Eric's!" is a phrase I often here from ambitious young girls. They have stars in their eyes when they read of the sweet, romantic way Eric proposed to me or how beautiful our first kiss was on our wedding day. They look ahead and long for such beauty and romance to come their way. But all too often, they don't realize that it all begins with *heart surgery*. If Jesus Christ isn't Lord over this area of our lives, He can't be the center of our love life or help us to build a relationship that will last forever. We must not expect Him to bless us in this way unless we have made Him Lord.

Which barnyard animal best describes you today? Are you like the Little Red Hen who had the goal of making fresh bread and who was willing to go through the hard work, and struggle, and sacrifice to get it? Or are you more like the horse, and the pig, and the goat, and the cow who expected to enjoy the blessings of the bread but were totally unwilling to do what it took to make the bread happen? If you're going "moo-moo" or "oink-oink" right now, time to make some changes!

Eric and I didn't just wake up one day and decide to put together a godly relationship. It all started between us and God. It started with our *surrender* to Jesus Christ. You can't hire a contractor to come and build a house for you if you don't first have some property for him to build it on. He has nothing to work with! In the same way God must have the property of your soul and heart before He can begin to build a true godly love story.

How do you begin building a castle of dreams? By

surrendering *everything* to Jesus Christ. No, it's not the fun part. It's not the exciting part. It's NOT the romantic part, that's for sure. But without this foundation, God has nothing to work with. Surrender is an *extreme* act of trust in God. It isn't something to be taken lightly.

Legend has it that a great conqueror once sailed to an island with his men to conquer savage natives. Once they landed on the island, they realized they were facing more than they bargained for. The enemy was much stronger than they'd anticipated. The men realized they might be forced to retreat to their ship and sail for their lives. But the head of the expedition had different plans. He gave orders for their ship to be burned. He knew that if his men had no way of escape, they would fight hard enough to conquer the enemy.

No escape. No turning back. Surrender must be the same. You can't have one foot in the door of surrender, and one foot in the door of your own way. It's all or nothing! True surrender leaves no room for retreat. It's ceasing to struggle, and strive, and plot, and plan, and worry, and wonder.

Surrender is simply saying, "Lord, I am all Yours. I give this part of my life to You. You may do with me whatever you will. I'll wait for Your timing. I'll wait for Your best. I want You to be the author of my love story. From this day on, this is Your area—not my own."

Surrender isn't something you do once and it's over. Surrender is a daily commitment! You might start with a decision to wait for God's best in this area, but then you have to live that decision out in everyday life.

It's an act of surrender each time you discipline yourself not to date around like all your friends are doing.

It's an act of surrender each time you decide not to flirt with members of the opposite sex. It's an act of surrender each time you refuse to allow your mind to dwell on wrong thoughts about the opposite sex. No, it's not easy. But someday, each moment of sacrifice will turn into a piece of the beautiful gift God gives you in return for your acts of surrender. It's all worth it in the end!

The heart of true surrender was captured well by Laura, a twenty-year-old college student, in the words to the song that she wrote. Perhaps you're ready to make it your prayer . . .

I Surrender My Will

Laura Hart

Every day I'm faced with the choice of doing things
Your way or mine;
But when I do it my way, I always seem to find
Your ways are better, Your vision is stronger,
And You only want what's best for me.

So I surrender my will to You.
I surrender my will to You, Lord.
I surrender my will; I give You my life.

There are times when my will demands to take control.
I fight to do things alone; but I always wake to find
Your path is better, Your sight for me is broader,
And You only want what's perfect for me.

So I surrender my will to You.
I surrender my will to You, Lord.
I surrender my will; I give You my life.

When times get harder, my soul grows weaker.
My heart gets tired, and I can't do it on my own . . .

So I surrender my will to You.
I surrender my will to You, Lord.
I surrender my will; I give You my life.

Chapter 6
Super Bowl Blues

Eric

*L*ooody! Loooody!" they chanted as I strolled into the cafeteria that fateful night in January. It seemed the entire college campus knew that I was eating humble pie. "Looody! Loooody!" The taunting continued, and my face turned a shade of red that rivaled Superman's cape.

I had put my faith in the Denver Broncos. I had stuck my neck out on the line for them, and they had let me down. Everyone seemed to know that I was the resident Bronco football fanatic, and everyone wanted to let me know how mistaken I had been to put my trust in them. They didn't just lose, they were chewed up and spit back out. And I, their most faithful follower, was pondering denying I ever lived in Denver, Colorado as the crowd chanted, "Looody! Loooody!"

I wasn't just a Bronco football fan, I was a Bronco-maniac! I would dream in orange and blue and faithfully blow out my voice by the fourth quarter of each of their games. Posters of my heroes lacquered my walls, and even my bedspread reminded me of my allegiance. But this great defeat stuck a nail in my bandwagon tire. I found myself depressed. It was difficult to see meaning in what life was all about. After all, the Broncos had lost their fourth Super Bowl! Could there be a light at the end of this dark tunnel?

It was right at this time that God broke through to my heart. He knew that I was a hurting little boy, disappointed in my heros, disillusioned with my team. He seemed to sit down next to me and tenderly wrap His arm around my shoulder.

"So, your team blew it today, didn't they?" He softly spoke as if He understood my suffering.

"Yeah!" I grunted while staring dejectedly at the floor.

"You really believed in them, didn't you?" He sympathized.

"Sure did!" I muttered while fighting off the temptation to rip up my posters.

"Well, Eric," He whispered gently to my heart, "did you know you can continue to put your trust in the Denver Broncos, but they will let you down every time?"

I looked up at him through my battered emotions, curiously wondering what He was about to tell me.

"But Eric!" He continued. "If you put your trust in *Me*, I'll never let you down—and I will *always* win!"

There are times in our walk with God that He brings us to a breaking point. It's in these places that we realize we have been misplacing our affections, misdirecting our loyalties, and even forgetting what this life is really all about. In these precious times, it seems God becomes crystal clear to our heart. We recognize that our lives truly do belong to Him. And in these times, we are given a choice!

"God," I pleaded as I felt Him tug upon my heart, "why does it always seems like You are asking me to give up all these things in my life that everyone else gets to keep?"

I just knew He was wanting more of my life. In fact, I was quickly coming to understand He was wanting *all* of me. This time, He was knocking on a door in my heart that led to the room entitled "Ludy Pride." It was in this room that I had learned to dress to impress, to talk like a charmer, and to walk like a hunk. All my masks had been created in this room. My "I've got it all together" mask, my "Ladies Man" mask, my "Tough Older Brother" mask, and even my "Cool Dude" mask all originated in this one room.

"But God!" I bellowed as I pondered my future as a resident of Dorksville. "If I give up all of this, what will I

become? I mean, I've already given up the Denver Broncos to You. What would be left of me but a nerd without a life?"

I always seem to wrestle with God when He brings me to those breaking points. He started back in 1990 with just my willingness to identify with His Name. Then He moved on to the area of sports, and from there began to tinker with my "Ludy pride." His objective was (and still is) to mold me into His very likeness. It was as if He would extend His hand out to me and beckon me to entrust my life to Him. By His grace, I would give these areas of my life over to Him and soon discover a new freedom and a new beauty in living. But every once in a while God steps across the line and asks for something that He has no business asking for.

When God began to knock on the door in my heart which led to the room entitled "Relationships with the Opposite Sex," I got belligerent.

"No way!" I screamed. "NO WAY!!!"

Now, for quite some time, I had been feeling that God was pushing His limits. I mean, He had been asking me to do things I never heard of Him asking *anyone* else to do. For some reason, when God knocked on this sacred door in my heart, I found that I was not in the mood for discussion.

"God, this is *my* area!" I passionately reasoned. "Relationships are something that I care far too much about to just go tossing them into Your hands!"

I was a die-hard romantic who had spent many hours daydreaming about the "perfect" love story. Over the past eight or so years I had done innumerable studies on the female species and had deduced, down to the shoe size, what my future wife was going to look like. Giving this all up to God would be like spilling soy sauce onto a banana split. It would surely ruin everything!

I knew that if I entrusted this area of my life to God's control, one of two things would happen. Either I would be doomed to a life of singleness, or I would be sentenced to a life married to "THE BEAST!" I had been to church, and I had seen the type of people God was attracted to. There were some really funny looking ones mixed into that bunch.

The entire time I resisted God, I was failing to recognize one thing. God wasn't out to get me, He was out to bless me! If I could have somehow taken a peek into His loving Father's heart, I would have known that to lay my life completely in His hands would be the wisest thing I could ever do.

♡ ♡ ♡

We all hold on to things in our lives, determined not to lose control. Like little toddlers we cling to our toys unwilling to allow our tenderhearted Daddy to take them from our hands so that He can grant us something so much more beautiful—and so much more lasting. We need to learn to cherish these times of God's taking and learn to trust that the One who takes is also the very One who gave up everything on our behalf. He doesn't take for His benefit, but for ours!

Is there anything that I am holding onto that I am unwilling to give up? This is a prayer that most of us are scared to pray. We are afraid to lose control of the steering wheel of our lives. But if we knew His character, we would actually *want* to pray this prayer.

While I was in college, God led me to surrender to Him everything from the Denver Broncos to all the Cindy McFarlanes in my life.

God may lead someone else to give up the Beatles and

pumpkin pie. Each one of us secretly struggles for the position of control in our lives, and we have different things that must be surrendered into the gracious hand of our God.

Most of us can swallow the idea of surrendering our homework to God, but which of us is eager to give him our popularity, our friendships, our appearance—or how about our music? Surrendering is the cement of our castle. When Christ, the Solid Rock, is the basis of everything in our lives, it's then we are secure and unshakable.

I remember once when my mom interrupted me right in the middle of a Denver Bronco game. I was screaming and yelling, hooting and hollering, and my mom simply said, "Eric, if you get that excited for football, just think how excited you should be getting for Jesus!"

Those words lodged in my memory and haunted me for years. It wasn't until Jesus sat me down for our little chat about my football mania that I realized that I had been misplacing my affection and misdirecting my loyalties. I had Someone who would never let me down, a True Hero who had given His very life in my stead. I had something in my life worth cheering about, something even worth dying for. Jesus was Someone who had given His all to me. The least I could possibly do would be to give Him my all in return.

Surrendering to Jesus is the most logical thing in all of life. He created us, and He knows what is best for us. In the area of relationships with the opposite sex, we can so easily doubt His credibility. We forget that He knows every little detail about our lives. We are afraid He won't know what we are attracted to, but He is the One who gave us our gift of attraction in the first place.

Success in relationships begins with Jesus at the center

of both lives, leading both lives, and expressing love through both lives. Surrendering this area is very scary. But we just have to remember that He is more interested in this area of our lives than even we are.

If we desire to build a castle of dreams, we must first lay the concrete. Until we seriously deal with God and allow Him to take the steering wheel, we won't be ready to start building. We must challenge our hearts with three poignant questions:

1. Am I willing, if God so chooses, to remain single, with Christ alone as my spouse?

2. Am I willing, if God so chooses, to be married and to allow Him to do the matchmaking?

3. Am I willing, if God so chooses, to be married and to allow Him to determine the timetable?

Romance God's Way starts with laying your life completely in His gracious hands. The concrete is never exciting and it's always gray, but the castle that will follow is scrumptiously beautiful.

The remainder of this book hinges upon how you respond right now within your heart. If you're willing to allow God His rightful place in your life, you will discover romance beyond your wildest dreams. It's only when we place the pen in His hand that He can compose for us our very own whimsical romantic tale.

Commit your way to the LORD,
Trust also in Him, and He will do it.
Psalm 37:5 NASB

Lord, in my heart, I now build an altar to You. On it I lay my dreams, my desires, the things I've been holding onto so tightly. I've been afraid to let You have control. I've been trying to be the one in control. I now relinquish my rights to You. I give myself completely to You.

You may do with my life whatever You see fit. My life is completely in Your hands from now on. Not my will, but Yours be done. I surrender everything to You now, Lord Jesus. Forgive me for trying to hold on.

Chapter 7
Is God an Old Geezer?

Leslie

*I*magine you are standing at the altar on your wedding day as the pastor reads the vows in a deep monotone. Beads of sweat form on your brow as you realize that there is *no* turning back. You'll be with this person for the rest of your life!

You glance at the one by your side who is soon to be your spouse. Your heart sinks, and you look away. You don't have an ounce of attraction to this person's arid personality, and even less to the Hitler-like mustache below his bulbous red nose. You feel dismal and hopeless as you realize that you are about to commit to this person forever. You think back to how you got yourself into this mess in the first place.

I remember! It all started when I surrendered this area of my life to God! I just knew He would mess things up. Now my whole life is ruined, and I'm stuck with THE BEAST—forever!

Tears of frustration well up in your eyes as the pastor continues the ceremony. Your mate-to-be beams back, assuming your tears are for joy. You sigh remorsefully. Your only consolation is that you know you are doing the "spiritual" thing. But you aren't sure if you can really stand to live with someone whose breath smells like moldy sauerkraut!

Why didn't I just stick it out in the dating scene? you wonder.

The pastor is saying something that brings you back to reality. "Does anyone object to the marriage between this man and woman today?"

Finally you've can't take it anymore. You've had enough. "Yes!" you blurt out to everyone's shock. "I object!! How could God do this do me? He's ruined me!!! I don't care if I did surrender to God once, now I'm taking it back!"

You march back down the aisle as the guests gasp and

murmur and stare. Great Aunt Matilda is so flabbergasted she passes out cold in the second pew. The organ player gets flustered and begins to play the recessional at super high speed, and the bridesmaids get so confused they begin to throw the rice at each other. Your parents just shake their heads, too humiliated to even acknowledge you.

The minister who had been performing the ceremony announces his decision to ex-communicate you from the church just as reporters from the local paper rush in to capture the chaotic scene on film for the front page of tomorrow's paper.

You run out to the churchyard and realize that your life has hit rock bottom. And all because you "surrendered" the area of romance to God way back when.

Ever had that nightmare? You're not alone. I used to have it all the time when I first began to grapple with the issue of surrendering relationships to God. In the back of my mind, I knew surrender was the right thing to do, but I had a sinking feeling that God would destroy me by sending me a husband whom I couldn't stand but who was *very* spiritual. That's a common misconception about our Heavenly Father.

As we've spoken with hundreds of young people, we've seen that Satan has tricked them into believing the same lies we once did about what happens when they surrender to God in this area.

Misconception #1
THE BIG OLD MEANIE GOD

God is out to get you, right? He's up there in Heaven right now just waiting to pounce on you. The moment you

say, "I surrender to You, Lord," He rubs His hands together, laughs wickedly, and says, "Aha! I got ya'!"

Next He lays on the rules just to make your life miserable.

"Okay, Susie. Now that you've surrendered to Me, you've got to do what I say or I'll send fire and brimstone down from Heaven to devour you instantly. It's time to make some serious changes in your life. From now on you must wear only long, gray dresses that come all the way to the floor. You must lock yourself in your room and come out only when absolutely necessary.

"Dump all of your friends; no more fun! The only people you are allowed to see are your immediate family members.

"You shall not lay eyes on a member of the opposite sex. We can't have you falling into temptation in any way. You can meet your future husband only on your wedding day. And, by the way, he will be someone you cannot stand, and your wedding will take place when you are about forty-five years old."

People who think that this is what God is like have a VERY difficult time surrendering to Him. And we don't blame them! Who wants to surrender to some mad scientist who only wants to wreck your life?

Misconception #2
THE OLD FOGEY GOD

God just doesn't get it, does He? I mean, sure He was really smart to be able to create the whole world and everything, but that was centuries ago! Now He's way past His prime and at least 2,000 years behind the times! He's just not clued in!

Can't you just picture what it would be like to surrender to that kind of God . . .

Tommy: Lord, I surrender this area of relationships to You.

God: Eh? What's that? Speak a little louder, Sonny!

Tommy: I SURRENDER TO YOU!

God: Eh? Oh . . . surrender, eh? Well, now that's just great. Surrender what?

Tommy: I'll let You pick out my wife.

God: What? You're looking for strife? Now why would you want strife?

Tommy: NO! My WIFE!!!

God: A wife, huh? Well, Sonny, I used to do a lot of matchmaking when I was younger. Got pretty good at it, too! Adam and Eve, Isaac and Rebecca, Mary and Joseph . . . Yes, sir! I was quite a happenin' guy back then! But Sonny, I'm gettin' older. I don't have the same kind of energy. Besides, my eyesight has gotten poor. I can't tell a blonde from a brunette these days. But Sonny, just because you want me to find you a wife, I'll say yes.

Now what is it that boys are attracted to these days? Oh, yes! Bloomers and beehive hairdos! Well, let me think. I know of one young lady named Atilla who might suit you. Of course, she's a good twenty years older than your mother, but you won't mind that, will you? You'll have to be patient though; I don't move as fast as I used to. With luck, I'll be able to get to it in say, thirty years or so.

Tommy: Thirty years?!!!

God: And now, Sonny, I need to go take a little snooze. I'm not as young as I used to be, you know! Oh! My achin' back!

Who wants to surrender to a God who has no clue what your needs and desires are?

Misconception #3
THE WORKAHOLIC GOD

God is way too busy to bother with your love life, isn't He? I mean, look at all the things He has to take care of in the world. He'd rather just let you pick this person out yourself and then put His stamp of approval on the romance once you've found Mr. or Miss Right. The truth is He doesn't really care who you marry as long as he or she is a good, moral person. You can just hear Him responding to your prayer for a future spouse.

"What, Katie? Wait a second, let me put you on hold. I'm getting a fax from South Africa." (Pause as angel-choir "hold" music plays for sixty seconds.)

"Okay, I'm back. Now what's this all about? Your future husband? You want me to find him for you? Uh, Katie, I hate to break this to you, but I just don't know if I can squeeze in a job like that . . . Wait a second, here comes an emergency call from the Middle East. Hold on." (Another thirty seconds passes as more angel-choir music comes on.)

"Okay, Katie. Now listen. I'd like to help you out here, but I'm dealing with five wars, abortion, gang violence, poverty, world hunger, and trying to save the rain forests all at once. Plus, this is election year and I've got a big mess at the White House I've got to deal with. I'm in way over my head! I'll tell you what I'll do. I'll connect you with my secretary. Maybe she can squeeze you into my appointment book in about ten years. Okay?

"Oh, listen. I've gotta cut this call short. As you can hear, all of our fifteen million fax lines are ringing, and my angel staff is really overworked. Next time try to contact me on e-mail, okay?"

Who wants to surrender to a God who has no time or interest in your love life?

We need to know who God really is before we can surrender this area of our lives to Him. We need to understand His nature and His character. A big part of the surrendering process is TRUST. To trust in who our God is. To trust that He is in complete control, that He does care about this area of our lives, and that His plans for us are AWESOME! *God loves romance!!* He *isn't* out to get us. He's *not* behind the times. And He's certainly *not* too busy to take charge of this part of our lives.

He knows us better than we know ourselves. He created us! And that means He created the unique attraction gift within us. He knows who we're attracted to! And He knows our every dream and desire! When He brought Adam and Eve together, they were perfectly suited for each other in every way. And He wants to do the same for each one of us.

Psalm 37:4 (NIV) says, "Delight yourself in the LORD and he will give you the desires of your heart." The fact is, He *loves* to give good gifts to His children!

When God brought Eric and I together, we were so amazed at how much we felt His Father's heart of delight in our love. He created a pure and beautiful romance between us—a romance so much more thrilling than anything we could have tried to create ourselves.

We realize, looking back, that all the while we had been dating around, searching for fulfillment in this area, He was right there all the time, just waiting to give us this gift of

pure, godly love. And when we finally surrendered, it was as if He said, "Just wait till you see the amazing plans I have in store! I can't wait to write this love story! I'm going to make all your dreams come true!" And we stood back and watched in amazement as He did just that!

Some say, "That's okay for you because it was His will for you to be married, but what if His plan is for me never to get married? How can I trust Him then?"

Remember, God only wants what's best for each of us. No matter what He calls us to, He has our highest good in mind. He will give us the grace AND the desire to face His plan, even if it is different than what we think right now would be best. No matter what, if we trust Him, we will undoubtedly look back and declare, "God ways are perfect!"

Trust in the LORD with all your heart
and lean not on your own understanding;
in all your ways acknowledge him,
and he will make your paths straight.
Proverbs 3:5–6 NIV

Lord, forgive me for not trusting You. For believing You to be anything other than completely good and loving and all-powerful. I realize that You only want what's best for me. Your ways are not my ways, but Your ways ARE best. When the road ahead gets rocky and I want so much to take matters into my own hands, help me remember Your lovingkindness and continue to trust. You are faithful. Never let me forget Your unfailing faithfulness.

I Place My Life Into Your Hands
Leslie Ludy

Lord, I am holding on so tightly.
I need You to come help me see.
Touch my eyes to see who You are;
Help me trust You completely.
What is my life but a breath for You to use somehow;
What do I really deserve?
You owe me nothing. I owe You everything;
So Lord, from this day forth my life is Yours.

I place my life, I place my will,
I place my heart into Your hands.
All that I am, all of my dreams,
All that I ever hope to be, I now lay them at Your feet.
You can do with me what You will;
My life is in Your hands.

Sometimes I catch a glimpse of who You really are
And who I am in light of You.
Lord, every breath I take,
Every heartbeat is nothing at all apart from You.
What is my life but a breath for You to use somehow;
What do I really deserve?
You owe me nothing. I owe You everything;
So Lord, from this day forth my life is Yours.

I place my life, I place my will,
I place my heart into Your hands.
All that I am, all of my dreams,
All that I ever hope to be, I now lay them at Your feet.
You can do with me what You will;
My life is in Your hands.

Your Castle of Dreams . . . Update

Good work! Nice cement pouring! What's next on the work schedule? Well, what does every castle have around it to protect it from invasion? That's right, a moat!

A moat is a trench you dig around the entire castle and fill with plenty of water and alligators to munch on any unwelcome visitor who tries to break in. Only those favored few whom you choose to lower the drawbridge for may enter your castle . . . and hopefully you will save that drawbridge entrance only for your future spouse.

STEP 2: Digging the moat. Translated into relationships that means—

inward purity.

Chapter 8
Dateless on a Friday Night?

Eric

*G*ulp! the delicious remains of my ice cream cone slid down my throat. I wiped the crumbs off my shirt as the fumes of disappointment filled my mind like exhaust fills the nostrils. *It will cost me another eighty-five cents to get another one,* I sadly calculated. In college eight-five cents was a lot of money, which made it difficult to justify even an extra chocolate-vanilla swirl cone on a Friday night.

I turned my attention back to the conversation around the plastic yellow table. My college buddies and I were escaping the books and living it up that night in the local McDonald's. It was anathema to discuss homework. We were out to have fun! As we gulped down the remains of our "weekly rewards," the discussion drifted from food, football, and fast cars . . . to girls.

Girls?! my mind yelped for joy. *I love to talk about girls!!!* The subject of girls had been a favorite of mine since the Cindy McFarlane days way back when I was stricken with puberty.

There was a lot of laughter, a few sighs, even tears as some-one mentioned the fact that we were all dateless on a Friday night. As I wiped the tear from my eye, my mind drifted far and away from the conversation around the plastic yellow table to the little chat I had with God a couple months prior.

Wait a minute, Eric! I reprimanded myself. *You gave this area of your life to God, remember?* There was half of me that remembered, and another half of me that refused to be historical and to reminisce that night.

Surgeon God had done some deep work in my life since the amputation in the area of relationships had been completed. I had surrendered my control, at the risk of Him

doing whatever He desired with this precious part of my existence. But instead of God gleefully cackling, "Now I've got you!" He seemed to gently assure me that He was going to bless me beyond my imagination if I continued to trust Him.

Now hold on, Eric! part of me beckoned. *Don't you recall that God assured you He had someone very special picked out just for you?* This seemed to awaken the reticent part of me that was still struggling with the "trusting God" thing. God *had* assured me that He was setting apart a princess just for me.

My buddies could have been talking about Canadian bacon and pineapple pizza, and I wouldn't have heard them. I was in "La-la Land" pondering the fact that *if* it was true that God was saving a lovely lady just for me, *She's probably alive right now!* I had never really considered that. Unless I was twenty years older than her, she was roaming the earth right that very minute. My mind could not be stilled.

Well, if she's alive right now, I wonder where she is on this terrestrial ball? In a boat on Lake Michigan? In a bagel shop in Jerusalem? Riding an elephant in Zaire? For all I know, she could be running around in a diaper in Newark, New Jersey!

I didn't know what color hair she had, the sound of her voice, the color of her eyes—let alone her date of birth. But for the first time in my life, I was recognizing the fact that she was most likely "out there somewhere."

She's out there somewhere! my mind excitedly cheered. Then I had an ominous thought. *I wonder what she is doing right now?* A lightning bolt of panic struck me as I pondered the possibilities of where she might happen to be right at that

very moment. *Wait a minute!* I said to myself. *It's a Friday night. . . What if she's . . . No! NO! It can't be true!* My brain bawled. *She better not be . . . with . . . a GUY?*

I could not escape the fact that it was a Friday night, a full moon, and if I had *my* druthers, *I'd* be spending it with a girl. After I had overcome the horrible shock of such a thought, an even worse idea slipped into my mind like ice down the back of my shirt.

No! No!! NEVER! I snorted inside my reverberating cranium walls. All I could picture in my gross imagination was some turkey wrapping his snake-like arm around the shoulders of my wife-to-be, slithering close with cologne dripping from his pores, puckering his unbridled oversized lips, and *smackeroo!* Laying one right on her!

My face reddened like a bruised tomato. My eyes blazed like sizzling craters. I plunged my fist into my open hand, pledging to wipe this guy off the planet like crumbs off my chin. I was furious! This conscienceless criminal was *kissing MY wife!!*

With the gentleness of a dove, God seemed to descend upon me. Amidst my raving lunacy, He somehow spoke to my heart. *Eric, you desire purity in your wife, don't you?*

You better believe it, God! She's gonna be pure! I hollered back inside my head. *Please, God! Give me a revelation of this guy's address so I can introduce him to an early grave!*

So tenderly He responded to me. He seemed to quietly say, *Eric, that's good that you desire her purity. But just think! If you desire purity in her, how much more do you think she desires purity in . . . YOU?*

I'll never forget that Friday night. I don't know what my buddies thought of my little tirade, but I didn't care. My mind and heart were consumed with what it meant to be pure.

Growing up, purity had always meant not having sex before marriage. I figured if I was a virgin when I got married, I would surely be deemed *pure*. I never once thought of purity in any other way until that fateful Friday night.

When thinking about getting married someday, there is something—sort of an unnamed and unmentioned commitment—that floats through every Christian young person's brain. I call it the "purity bargain." The purity bargain is that unspoken agreement, between two people who have never met, that goes something like this: *You keep yourself pure for me, and I just might keep myself sort of pure for you.*

I had always wondered if my wife would keep her end of the "purity bargain," but I admit that I'd never really considered that my end of the agreement was a little shady. I wanted my wife to never have laid eyes on a member of the male species, yet I wanted to "prepare" myself for marriage with a healthy dose of "interaction" with members of the opposite sex. It was while sitting around that plastic table in McDonald's that I realized my end of the "purity bargain" needed to be rewritten. Rewritten to favor my wife instead of myself. Because that's God's way.

I developed a purity test for myself. I imagined that the eyes of my wife-to-be were watching me. I would ask myself, "If she could see me now with this girl, how would she feel?" I determined that if she would feel hurt, jealous, or even disappointed, then something was not right with how I was "relating."

I realized the most amazing truth . . . I had a LOVE LIFE even then—before I ever met her. I had to choose either to love her, or to love myself, day in and day out. If she really was watching me, then I would want her to feel cherished and adored by the way I was living my life. If the

words I was speaking or the way I was living was not showing love to her, then I wasn't keeping up my end of the revised purity bargain:

> *I must keep myself pure for her no matter what she does for me, because in doing that I'm modeling the amazing and unconditional love of Jesus Christ.*

We hear a lot of talk today about abstinence. I think that is wonderful! But as Christians we must realize that Jesus isn't impressed with just our external purity, He's interested in what is going on *inside*. Most of us never consider that if our thought life was recorded for our future spouse to read, he or she would be shocked and horrified, insulted and mortified, when they read the first few sentences.

Purity involves our entire self—mind, heart, and body. When we only consider our physical virginity, we forget that the treasure of purity God has given us is kept polished and protected by the choices we make that nobody but God can see. Jesus said during His Sermon on the Mount:

> *"You have heard that it was said, 'Do not commit adultery.' But I tell you that anyone who looks at a woman lustfully has already committed adultery with her in his heart"* (Matthew 5:27–28 NIV).

Purity is a serious issue to God! When He was down here on this earth, the people that got under His skin were the ones that only valued external purity and, in doing so, forgot about purity of the heart and mind. In fact, it could be said that Jesus would have fallen head over heels in love with the Pharisees if He were only interested in what we as humans do on the outside. The Pharisees were immaculately pure on the

outside, but Jesus called them "whitewashed tombs!" In other words, they were rotting on the inside. God is interested in purity in the innermost parts.

When we choose to guard our every thought and keep our passionate emotions just for the "special someone" that God has picked out for our lives, we are, in a sense, loving them even now. We are prizing them above ourselves. We are modeling Christ's love for them as we selflessly give up our personal desires to grant them theirs.

If you desire to build a castle of dreams, you must hollow out a moat. A moat is one of those big trenches around the outside of the castle that is filled with murky water and alligators. It is used to keep outside invaders away so that the castle may remain under the rightful authority. By keeping ourselves pure, we are in a sense doing that very thing. We are guarding the treasure that God has given us by turning away the temptations that can so quickly erode our foundation.

Purity is a choice! It is a decision that must be made every day, all day long. It's not something like eating an ice cream cone, and it's a whole lot more costly than eighty-five cents. It's not easy, and we definitely can't stay pure in our own strength. Our only hope for purity is the Pure One Himself—Jesus Christ.

If you are anything like me, you've blown it. Purity is a thing of the past, and hopelessness is the feeling of the present. But just remember what the Pure One has done on our behalf. No matter how much dirt we have rolled around in, He is ready to wash us completely clean. Because of His death, He has given us hope for a future full of

purity—*His purity*. The decisions we have made will always be with us, but God, in His grace, will turn them for our good if we choose to walk His way from this day forward.

One of the most difficult things I ever had to do was tell Leslie about all the Cindy McFarlanes I gave my mind, heart, and body to. In my journal I called it, "The Night I Hung My Underwear Out to Dry." I thought for sure she would hate me for what I had given away that I should have been saving for her. But I'll never forget her beautiful response. "Eric, I forgive you," she said tenderly and sweetly while tears of sorrow streamed down my face. She forgave me! It hurt her deeply, but she forgave me!

A while later, before our wedding, Leslie shared with me a desire of her heart. "Eric, I wish that you never had a thought for another girl but me in your entire life." As ridiculous as I thought that desire was at the time, God showed me so much through it.

First of all, I had been right in thinking that Leslie would desire purity in me even before I met her. And secondly, if Leslie desired such faithfulness and purity, how much more does my gracious God in Heaven?

Purity cannot be measured by human technology. It can only be measured by God. The choice to pursue purity is a decision that you must first make between you and God. It's impossible *without* Him, yet it's only natural *with* Him.

"I have made a covenant with my eyes
not to look lustfully at a girl."
Job 31:1 NIV

Cleanse me, Lord. I have allowed my mind to dwell on lustful thoughts toward the opposite sex. I know this is as adultery in Your eyes. Forgive me, Lord. I have allowed my heart and emotions to be defiled and given away in relationships You never intended me to be in. I have traded in my treasure of purity for the sake of my own temporary pleasure or security. This breaks Your heart. Forgive me, Lord.

From now on, help me walk in purity. Help me learn to guard my thoughts, my heart, my emotions, my body, that I would honor You and my future spouse from this day forward.

Your Castle of Dreams . . . Update

You've got a great foundation! You've even got a nice moat around your castle filled with plenty of alligators. What's next? Time to work on the grounds.

Your castle needs to be surrounded with plenty of woods, mountains, ponds, streams . . . You don't want it right in the middle of New York City. You need some privacy!

Start planting the seeds for a forest around your castle. When that special someone does come along, he or she will truly appreciate what you have been saving just for him or her! Besides, if your castle is secluded, you won't have to listen to all the busy-bodies who would stand around and give you bad advice while you are trying to build. By surrounding yourself with woods, you won't be distracted by anything else. You will be able to take your directions only from the Master Designer Himself. So start planting!

STEP 3: Build your castle in "a land far away." Translated into relationships that means—

waiting on God.

Chapter 9
Tunnel Vision

Leslie

God, I surrender this area of my life to you!" you dramatically proclaim. "I won't go out and look for a relationship, I will wait patiently for Your perfect timing." Feeling great about your new commitment and full of confidence in God's "perfect timing," you settle back and make yourself comfortable. You are sure that this "waiting-not-dating" theory will work great for you. A full minute passes. You sigh and smile. *This waiting stuff isn't so hard after all!* you remark to yourself. Five minutes goes by. *Wow! There's just nothing to this! It's really simple!*

After about twenty minutes, you begin to get slightly fidgety so you move to the window and stare out. *Yep,* you tell yourself, *this is the way to go! Just sit back and relax and let God do all the work. My future spouse could be on my doorstep any minute now.*

At the thirty minute mark you start pacing back and forth. "Um . . . excuse me? God? It's me again. I just wanted to make sure that you knew I'm down here WAITING for you to do something in this area of my life. Remember? At 6:00 this evening I made a commitment to wait on You for my future spouse. And . . . uh . . . I don't mean to be rude or anything, but I've been waiting for a full thirty minutes. I'm ready anytime You are, okay?"

Five more minutes drag by. Now you are really agitated. Tick, tock, tick, tock, tick, tock . . . The clock on the wall just keeps ticking, and the minutes slide by slowly. You check the window one more time. No sign of your future spouse yet. You heave a huge sigh and look at your watch. You decide to give God one more minute.

You watch the second hand move around the circle. When the time is up, you burst out in frustration, "God! Listen, how long do you expect me to sit here waiting for my future spouse?! It's been exactly *thirty-six* minutes! I

don't have all day, You know! I have people to see, places to go . . . I can't just sit here like a vegetable. Sorry, God, but this waiting stuff just doesn't work! I'm going back out to the dating scene. I can't waste time waiting around for You to get a move on."

Okay, okay. I know you aren't quite *that* impatient, but you have to admit, very few of us have any sort of an understanding of what it means to WAIT.

Waiting has become a *bad word* to us in this culture. We have grown up in a fast-food, fast-fun, fast-technology generation, and we don't know how to wait for anything. I mean, seriously, think about all the times you've rushed in the house starving, run into the kitchen, flung open the fridge, pulled out a plate of leftovers, and popped them into the microwave. As soon as you push the start button, you begin pacing the kitchen floor. *When is this stupid microwave going to finish cooking?* you wonder to yourself. You are actually pacing impatiently in front of a devise that is ultra-speed heating your lunch. How absurd!

When we hear the term, "Waiting on God for your future spouse" we panic. "Wait? For how long? What if God doesn't bring someone into my life until I'm some awful age like (horror of horrors) *thirty*? There's just NO WAY I can wait that long!"

Or we might respond by saying: "Waiting on God? But what do you DO when you 'wait on God'? Do you just sit around all day and hope that your future spouse just magically shows up on your doorstep?"

Surrender was hard enough . . . then came trust . . . now WAITING? When we picture ourselves waiting for

God to bring our future spouse into our lives, we think it's going to be like planting a seed in the ground and standing there staring at it until it finally grows into a flower. How boring! That would drive you nuts!

No wonder we get depressed when we hear the word *waiting*. We think of ourselves becoming a "spiritual couch potato" where we do nothing but sit around and stare, eyes glazed over, dismally watching our Bible (instead of the TV), sipping iced tea (instead of beer), and developing an unattractive "Bible belly" (instead of a beer-belly). Every now and then we belch out a few spiritual-sounding words, but our lives really amount to nothing. We wait in this condition for years and years until God *finally* decides to *DO something*!

Don't be fooled by first impressions. Waiting is anything BUT becoming a "spiritual couch potato." Waiting is an ACTIVE word. Waiting on God means energetic expectancy. You remember what it used to feel like the night before Christmas? You were so excited you could hardly sleep. You got tingles up your spine and butterflies in your stomach when you thought of what was going to happen the very next morning . . . Christmas! Presents! Food! Celebration!

"How early can I get up?" you asked your parents excitedly.

"You have to wait till 6 a.m.," they informed you.

"Six a.m.? That's late! How about 3 a.m. instead? I can't wait to open presents!"

You were jittery and expectant. You were sure that tomorrow was going to be a terrific day. Sure, the waiting was a little hard, but looking back you realize that it was all part of the fun.

That's a little like what it truly means to WAIT on God.

You just *know* He has an incredible plan. You are eager and expectant to see what that plan is. You share your excitement with Him. You watch. You listen. You remain alert and ready to see what He is going to do.

Some Important Keys to Waiting

1. Wait with a PURPOSE! Imagine this . . . You decide one day that you'd really like to go somewhere. You don't care where, just somewhere. So you put your jacket on and walk down the street. Eventually you come to a little red sign on the sidewalk that says, "Bus Stop." You decide to wait at the bus stop for a bus. Of course, you have no idea when the bus is coming or where it is going, but you somehow think that if you wait long enough, something will come pick you up. After an hour or two standing there, people begin to ask you what you are doing.

"I'm waiting for a bus!" you reply.

"You idiot! The bus only stops here on Fridays! This is Monday! Get a life!"

Dejected, you put your hands in your pockets and head for home, realizing you've just wasted most of your day waiting for something that was not going to come.

Okay, I know you are far too brilliant to ever do anything so stupid as to wait for a bus that wasn't coming, but think about that analogy in relationship to your spiritual life. Why wait for God's best when you don't even know WHAT you are waiting for?

The key is to hold on to God's promises. He has a beautiful plan for you! You are waiting for no less than His very best. In making the decision to wait on God, you are proclaiming, "I will *not* settle for anything less than the perfect will of God for my life. Though the world may

offer me many appealing options, only in waiting for His best will I truly be fulfilled." If God's plan for you is marriage, your future spouse is out there somewhere. When God finally brings him along, you will be able to say, "I have been waiting all my life for this moment!"

Have you ever heard the love songs on the radio with the ridiculous mushy lyrics? "I have been waiting all of my life for someone like you, ooh, ooh . . ." Liar! The jerk singing that song has probably had intimate relationships with at least fifty women in the past year. You call that "waiting"?! Give me a break!

True waiting involves FOCUS. You know what you are waiting for . . . God's best. Don't let *anything* distract you!

It's like walking through a tunnel. You can just get a glimpse of the brilliant rays of the sun at the end. Your goal is to get to that sun, but all along the sides of the tunnel are these little people yelling out to you with things to try to distract you from reaching the end of the tunnel. They are trying to convince you that they have options even better than the light of the sun.

"Hey, Danny, look at this!" one of them calls, holding something out to you. "I've got a fancy flashlight here, just for you. It would make this walk through the tunnel so much easier. You wouldn't have to trip over your own feet anymore. Just think how nice that would be. You wouldn't have to stare straight ahead to find your way out of this awful tunnel. All you need to do is come over and look at this flashlight. Really! It's a great buy! You *can't* do without it! It's made of real plastic and everything!"

You know that if you turn your head away even for a moment, you will lose the glimpse of the sun at the end of the tunnel. Getting to the true light is your goal, so you keep walking.

"Hi, there!" another one cries loudly as you approach. "I've got something for you. You're just gonna *love* me for this. It will save your life, man! It's a *genuine* electric torch. You'll *never* have to look ahead into that sunlight again. This will satisfy your desire both for heat and light. It not only gives off a glow that is just as bright as the real sun, you can also control the heat switch for added comfort as you travel through this terribly chilly tunnel. Hey man, who needs to get to the sun when you've got something just as good. Just come over here and take a look, boy!"

You have to keep looking straight ahead. You have to stay focused. If you take your eyes off the prize God has for you at the end of the tunnel, you will be distracted by the "toys" the world tries to offer you. If it ever seems that the temporary relationships the world can offer you NOW beats waiting for "God's best," you can take that as a warning sign that you are *not* focused on the end of the tunnel. If we could only see how awesome God's plans for us really are, we would never settle for the world's so-called pleasures. God's best *always* blows away the temporary pleasures of today. Stay focused! Keep your eyes on the goal!

2. Don't just sit there . . . PRAY! Pray for what? Your future spouse, of course! Feel kind of strange praying for someone whom you don't even know? Why? This is the person you are going to spend your entire life with . . . and he or she is most likely out there somewhere! Pray, pray, pray! Pray that God will protect that special person and help him or her stay focused on waiting for His best (you!) until He brings you together. Pray that He will mold your future spouse into exactly who He's created him or her to be.

I've heard several amazing stories of couples who prayed for each other long before they ever met. In one situation,

a group of people in a prayer meeting were prompted to pray for someone in danger. They felt led to intercede for two men in a small airplane over the Great Lakes area with little fuel and no place to land. The group offered up requests for their safety. Quite some time later one of the young women from the prayer meeting met her future husband and found out that he had been in the exact situation they had prayed for—flying with another man in heavy fog over the Great Lakes area, in danger because they had no place to land and were running out of fuel. At the last minute, a landing place had suddenly opened up, and the plane had come down safely.

As the young woman and her husband-to-be compared dates, they discovered that his plane adventure most likely happened close to the same time her group had prayed for the men in the airplane. God had stirred this young woman's heart to pray for the protection of her husband's life before she had even met him! Don't underestimate the power of prayer!

If you have read the beautiful story of how God brought Eric and I together, you remember that it all started with Eric lying on his back on a cold December evening, praying for his future wife. A picture popped into his head of a young lady with brown hair. He felt something say to his heart, *This is your wife!* She was a girl he had never seen before, and he really didn't believe this strange experience meant anything. But the very next night he was at a Christmas play and saw the same young lady walk out onto the stage, singing. And thus began our beautiful love story. But it really began with prayer. Eric had been praying for me for over a year. For some reason, lying on his back on that cold night in December was the appointed time for God to start moving. Don't give up! Prayer changes things!

3. **Wait FAITHFULLY.** Be committed to your future spouse not just physically, but emotionally as well. Guard your thoughts, especially toward members of the opposite sex. What good is it to have waited and waited for your spouse only to have spent that time consumed with lustful and wrong desires towards others? You are setting yourself aside in *every* way for this person. On your wedding day, you want to be able to offer him or her the absolute purity of your body, mind, and heart.

Keep reminding yourself that faithfulness to your marriage partner begins right now—not just after you are married. Believe me, if you start practicing faithfulness now, faithfulness *after* marriage will come naturally.

I will never forget when, on our honeymoon, Eric showed me pages and pages of letters, poems, and prayers he had written for me before he even knew me. He was practicing faithfulness to me for years before we met, and now I have confidence in his commitment to me! I KNOW what foundation our marriage is built upon.

It's okay to have friendships with the opposite sex in this time of waiting. But keep your mind and heart in check. Keep God as your focus, and don't be distracted by anything else.

Sometimes young people ask us, "But if I'm not consumed with the opposite sex, how will God be able to show me when he or she *is* the right one? I don't want to miss that person just because I'm not looking!"

Don't worry. You can't go wrong when you focus on God and choose NOT to be distracted by the opposite sex. When God wants to get your attention, He'll find a way to do it. If He has to trip you to get you to see His will, you can be sure He will be there to catch you and to point you

in the right direction.

It's a lot safer to treat ALL your friendships as if there is no possibility of a relationship developing. If God wants to change that, let Him. But if you leave doors of possibility open, it's easy to have relationships form that God didn't intend—relationships that will distract you from seeking His BEST for your life.

It's funny to look back on my friendship with Eric. We were so careful *not* to treat our friendship as anything more than a sister-brother relationship, that even when God began to do something more between us, it took us both a while to acknowledge it. I remember driving home in that memorable "mini-van" on the way back from New Orleans. We knew that God was doing something different in our friendship, but we just weren't quite sure what it was.

"I really want to be careful in our friendship," Eric said to me. "If your future husband came into your life right now, I wouldn't want to hinder your relationship with him because we are spending so much time together. And also, I want to honor and respect my future wife. If she came into my life right now, I wouldn't want her to feel jealous because I was spending time with you."

Eric and I talked about these "other people"—our future spouses—although in the back of our minds we both realized as we looked at each other that we could be looking at our future spouse. Until we were sure, however, we weren't going to entertain that possibility. And as you know if you've read the whole story, God went out of His way to get our attention when He really wanted us to know.

Wait in absolute faithfulness. Have more than just a few years of "not dating" to offer to your spouse someday.

Have the gift of your entire self—body, mind, and heart. It's a gift worth waiting to give!

I waited patiently and expectantly for the Lord,
and he inclined to me and heard my cry.
Psalm 40:1 AMP

♡ ♡ ♡

Forgive me for being discontented and impatient, Lord. I know that You know the timing that is best for me to be in a relationship. Help me to wait with an attitude of joy and expectation. Help me to be faithful in praying for my spouse and in preparing myself for that relationship. Teach me patience, Lord.

Your Castle of Dreams . . . Update

What do you have going for you? A great foundation, a lovely moat, and a nice, secluded forest surrounding your building site. Don't you think it's finally time to start building? Time to get those great big heavy blocks of stone and begin placing them on top of each other one by one until your castle is finished. It's time to roll up your sleeves.

STEP 4: The building blocks. Translated into relationship that means—

covenant love.

Chapter 10

Love...
Fleeting
or Forever?

Leslie

Oh I LOVE it!" you exclaim as you unwrap your birthday gift. You beam a winning smile to your parents, who knew just what was on the top of your "I want" list. You are thrilled and excited about the new ski outfit, or bike, or key to your own car, or whatever it is that they've just given you. Of course, your excitement dies down just a little as you open the next gift from Great Aunt Bertha. She has forgotten how old you are this year, but felt certain you were still young enough to enjoy a genuine hand-knit sweater with a lovely cross-stitch Bert & Ernie engraved on the front. Oh well, you have to LOVE her.

The next day you are at a friend's house, and you both decide to order pizza. Your friend is on the phone with Speedy Delivery Pizza Express, and the pizza man is patiently waiting for you to decide what kind of pizza you want. "How about anchovies for a change?" your friend brightly suggests.

"No way! Get pepperoni! I LOVE pepperoni!" you respond emphatically.

Finally after about five minutes of debating over this agonizing decision, you come to a compromise—half pepperoni, half anchovies. The pizza man is relieved to be off the phone with you two.

After a fun evening with your friend and your beloved pepperoni pizza, you drive home and have a brief conversation with your parents who are sitting at the kitchen table trying to plan a vacation getaway. Finally, your eyelids become droopy as you glance at all their brochures on Florida and the Caribbean. You decide to turn in. You head upstairs and call over your shoulder, "Goodnight Mom and Dad. I LOVE you!" As you drift off to sleep, you think to yourself, *Oh good, tomorrow is Saturday. I get to sleep in.*

I LOVE sleeping in!

LOVE . . . What does that word really mean? In our culture, the word *love* is the most overused word of all. Just think, in the last twenty-four hours you have used it to describe at least a dozen different things—from your birthday presents to pepperoni, to your Mom and Dad, to sleeping. And then, of course, you are supposed to use the same word to build your relationship with your future spouse upon. No wonder everyone is so confused!

If we are going to truly have a love life built by God, we need to understand His idea of what *love* means. Did you know that there are really three different types of love described in the Bible? I thought it might be fun to take a look at each.

Agape Love

Agape love . . . *a love that is based on commitment and not feeling; a love that sacrifices for the good of the other; the very love that Christ had for us when He died in our place.*

I once heard the story of a Christian man who was being tortured in a foreign prison camp because of His faith. His torturer, a wicked prison guard, was beating him mercilessly.

"Ha ha!" the guard sneered. "I have more power than the God you serve! I hold your life in my hands! I can determine whether you will live or die! I have all the power!"

"No," said the tortured man quietly, "that is not true. You can beat me, torture me, laugh at me, even kill me, but I still have one power which you don't have . . . I can *love* you. And nothing you can do, even in taking my life, can

make me stop loving you."

Wait a minute!? Hold on! Did you read that right? Did that man who was being tortured actually say he *loved* the prison guard who was about to kill him? How can that be. possible?

Agape love! It's not based on a feeling, but a choice. We always have the option to choose agape love—the kind of love that decides to consider the good of the other person above our own desires. That's the kind of love Jesus displayed as He died upon the cross for all of us. That's the kind of love we should have for all mankind. That kind of love is strong and solid. It's an act of the will.

Filial Love

Filial love . . . *the deep, kindred affection that we have for those we hold dear . . . our parents, our close friends; it's the kind of love that takes a special interest in seeing the other person succeed and be happy. It's a kind of love that cherishes the bond of friendship between two people. Filial love can only be attained after two people know each other very well.*

When my brother, John, was about twelve years old, he began to express "filial" love to each of his family members verbally. Whenever he would leave the house, he would call out to whoever happened to be there at the time, "Bye, Mom . . . love you!" or "Bye, Leslie . . . love you!" After a few months of this, it quickly became a habit.

One day, he was at Tae Kwon Do practice working toward his black belt. His teacher, Mr. Oberlander, was especially strict, stern, and unaffectionate towards all of his students. Before you blame him too much for that, I should

add that the sport of Tae Kwon Do is a very "serious" sport—full of proper etiquette, respectful manners, and strict rules. Needless to say, John had never had a very deep relationship with Mr. Oberlander. On this particular day, as he was leaving, he made a slip of the tongue.

"Bye, Mr. Oberlander . . . love you!" he blurted out as he was opening the door to exit. As soon as the words were out of his mouth, his heart dropped and his face turned beat red. Without looking back, he raced out to the car where I was waiting to pick him up. "Oh, I can't believe I did that!" he burst out. All the way home he chided and kicked himself. "Of all the things I could have said . . . See you later, have a nice day, see you next week . . . I had to say I LOVE YOU! I am soooo embarrassed!"

John sure made the trip home entertaining. I laughed so hard I could hardly drive. To this day, the "Mr. Oberlander" story is a family favorite.

Filial love is NOT something that can be felt toward just anyone. Why was saying "I love you" to Mr. Oberlander so backwards and hilarious? Because John did not share a deep friendship or affection with this man. It was only something he said to those that were very close to him.

Eros Love

Eros love . . . the romantic, emotional, sensual kind of love felt between a man and a woman. This is that "ooey-gooey" kind of love that turns even the toughest, most confident, individuals into idiots. Eros love is the tingling feeling you get when you hold hands with someone you're attracted to, or the spacey, day-dreamy feeling you get when you think about someone you can't wait to be with.

Eric has always been a very organized, meticulous, responsible type of person, but when the "eros love" kicked in to our relationship, all that temporarily disappeared. One night after we had taken a walk together, he drove home and was so out of it because of having been with me, that he parked the car at a crazy angle—half on the curb, half on the street—left the lights on all night so that the battery burned out, and left the front door ajar all night long. This is what eros love can do so, beware!

Now, look at the world around you. Out of those three types of love, which one do you think is what most couples begin with in their relationship? It's obvious, isn't it? Eros love—the "ooey-gooey" feeling you get when you see someone you're attracted to. Most relationships start because of eros love. The only problem is that eros love is so unsteady! It's like the wind—strong, gushing torrents one day and completely gone the next. It's like that Diet Pepsi, just one calorie, now-you-see-it-now-you-don't commercial. It can be here one day and gone the next. Eros love is a wonderful kind of love, but it is NOT a good foundation for a relationship that is going to stand the test of time.

Well, then, what kind of love *is* a good foundation to build a relationship on? You got it—agape love! Agape love is based upon a commitment, not a feeling. It doesn't come one day and disappear the next; it's a choice, an act of the will. Relationships that are built around agape love *will* stand the test of time, because agape love is the very love God has for us—strong and faithful and unchanging. When God begins to knit your heart with someone else's, filial love then eros love will follow to enhance and deepen the relationship. But only agape love is strong enough to last through eternity.

Most of us don't grow up with a desire to "get married

and then get divorced." Nevertheless, divorce is an epidemic raging throughout our Christian culture. Can we do anything to prevent divorce from plaguing our own lives? We can do a lot more than many people think to prevent divorce from happening. Let's start building our relationships on agape love instead of on feelings. Sure, the feelings are going to be a part of any love relationship—that's the fun part, but first a solid cornerstone *must* be laid.

Did you realize that you can begin showing agape love to your future mate *even now*? It doesn't matter if you don't know who he or she is. You can start laying the building blocks for your relationship with him or her right now! You already have a love life! How? By making choices each day to honor your future spouse and do what's best for him or her. Think about that relationship and learn to invest in it *now*, so that when that person comes along, you will already have a structure in place capable of housing a marriage that will last a lifetime.

Covenant Love

Covenant love . . . a*gape love toward your future spouse.*

There you are on your wedding day, listening to the pastor ask you the long-awaited questions. "Do you, Mike, pledge to love, honor, and cherish Diane, and to be faithful to her always—in plenty and in want, in sickness and in health, in good times and in bad, as long as you both shall live?"

"Hold on!" you quickly interject. "Pastor Smith, you're reading that wrong! Remember? I had my lawyer change the marriage contract to read, 'Do you Mike pledge to love, honor, and cherish Diane, and to be faithful to her always— as long as she cooks my steak medium rare, never gets over seven facial wrinkles or over twenty gray hairs, and always gives me first rights to the remote control.' Now get it right! I'm not going to say 'I do' to anything too unrealistic!"

A scenario like that sounds crazy! But sadly, most of the world sees the marriage agreement as something right along those lines. Many couples on their wedding day say "I do" to the pledge to be faithful no matter what, but deep in their hearts they are really saying, "I will love you as long as you are making me happy. Once you stop making me happy, we can seriously consider the option of divorce."

Marriage is meant to be a *covenant* not a *contract*. It's a relationship meant to last a lifetime, not just a few years.

If we base our relationship with our spouse on covenant love instead of the world's temporary kind of love, then we don't even have to worry about divorce. It no longer becomes an option.

Remember when Eric and I were on our honeymoon and he surprised me by reading all sorts of letters and poems he had written for me long before we'd ever met? They were things like, "I'm waiting for you. I wish you were here with me. I can't wait until God brings you into my life." I realized that even though at our wedding ceremony Eric and I had entered into a lifelong covenant together, his covenant love toward me actually started years ago. He had been faithful to me, making sacrifices and giving up temporary pleasures for the sake of investing in our relationship. This was all the more assurance to me that he would continue his faithfulness to me throughout the rest of our lives.

How can you tell the difference between a relationship built on covenant love and a relationship built on the world's

version of love? There is a huge difference between the two. Let's look at some telltale signs:

1. The world's love says "HURRY UP" . . . while covenant love is willing to WAIT for God's BEST.

You know the story. You see someone across the room at a party. They catch your eye. Wow! You are instantly attracted to them. As they move across the room toward you, your heart beats quicker. You just know this must be love at first sight. Once you start talking with them, you lose all track of time.

As you go home that night, all you can think of is being with them. The last thing on your mind is waiting. The last thing you want to do is pray about the situation, think it through, maybe talk it over with your parents. You want to just start dating this person! Why wait? You like them, they like you . . . let's go!

I once heard someone say, "The greatest enemy of the BEST is the GOOD, if only for the sake of time." How true! We get so excited about the GOOD things and want to jump right in, but all the while we miss the BEST things that would have come to us if we'd just waited a little bit longer.

In the book *Pilgrim's Progress* there is a brief story about two young kids in a nursery. Their names were Passion and Patience (this is the Ludy paraphrased version). They are brought into the nursery and promised some toys. Passion, true to his name, begins to kick and scream and throw a very annoying tantrum. "I want my toys now! Waaaaaa!" he yells at the top of his lungs. Now how long could you stand such irritating screams?

Well, the nursery workers couldn't stand it for very

long, so they finally brought him some toys, just to shut him up. Of course, they weren't the BEST toys, and so before long they break. Passion, of course, wants more toys, but it's too late for him. He already got his toys and no more will be coming.

Patience on the other hand, waits quietly (for what seems like a very long time) until they *finally* bring out his toys. Unlike Passion's toys, these are the BEST kind of toys that can be found. They *never* break, rust, or fall apart. Patience was willing to wait for the BEST, and in the end he was much happier because of it. A relationship built on covenant love *waits for God's very best!*

2. The world's version of love puts all value on what's on the OUTSIDE, while covenant love sees what's on the INSIDE as far more important.

Covenant love is NOT based upon what's on the outside. Covenant love sees that it's only what's on the *inside* of a person that will truly last forever.

I teach a girls' singing class in Denver. We often go to nursing homes to entertain and uplift the residents. It's amazing what happens when you get old. As I've observed these old folks, I've realized all the more clearly how fleeting beauty is. It simply doesn't last. I mean, how many times do you hear a young man say, "Whoa! What a babe!" when he sees an eighty-year-old lady walk by? It just doesn't happen. So it really is crazy to base love for someone upon something that only lasts a few years. What's on the inside, however, is what you take with you into eternity, whether it's bad or good.

One particular day when I was in a nursing home, I stopped by the room of a lady who was about eighty-nine years old. She was a former model, and on her dresser she had a picture of herself as she used to be—young and

beautiful. But now she looked just about the same as all the other ladies in the nursing home. She was frail, wrinkled, white-haired, and in a wheelchair. After a few minutes of talking with her, it was clear to me she had grown up putting all of her value on her external appearance. Now that had faded away, and her true character came out. She was griping and worrying and complaining about everything. She was mad about this and that. She was hardly capable of saying anything pleasant! I couldn't wait to get out of her room.

The next person I visited was the opposite. She was just as old and wrinkled as the former model, but it was obvious that she had lived her life putting more emphasis on who she was inside. She was sweet and pleasant and fun to talk with. I could have stayed with her all afternoon.

I decided right then and there that I wanted to live my life focusing more on *internal* character than *outward* beauty. At the end of my life, I wanted to have more to show than just a pretty picture on my dresser. I wanted a heart that was pure.

Covenant love goes so much deeper than the surface. Your future spouse won't always be as dazzlingly attractive as he or she is on your wedding day. But who cares? If your relationship is based on covenant love, you will love each other for what's on the INSIDE, and that is something that can grow more and more beautiful the longer you live!

3. The world's version of love is SELFISH. It asks, "What's best for ME?" while covenant love is always asking, "How can I serve the other person?"

Ladies, picture yourself in a crisis. A terrorist has just burst into your home with a machine gun and is threatening to kill everybody. Your husband screams with terror and jumps behind you, pushing you in front of him and yelling,

"Kill her first! She can take it!"

How many of you want to walk down the aisle with a man like that? Even though none of us would say we want that kind of character in our spouse, this is the basic attitude of most couples in a relationship. "What's in it for ME?" When they begin a dating relationship it is because they want to satisfy their longing for companionship. When they end a dating relationship, it is because the other person is no longer meeting their needs. This is NOT the attitude to take into a marriage that you expect to last. The only way a marriage will last is if both individuals decide to look at what is best for the *other* person, and not what's best for themselves.

When Christ died for us, He wasn't thinking of what would be best for Him. No, instead He sacrificed everything because that was what was best for *us*. This is the only attitude right for a lasting relationship. The very attitude of Christ.

We have a dear friend in Michigan named Karen. After about ten years of marriage, her husband was in a terrible car accident that left his brain severely damaged. From then on, he had to be taken care of like a child. He could no longer communicate with anyone on an adult level. He could no longer meet his wife's needs.

Most people wouldn't have blamed Karen if she had simply walked out of the marriage, put him in some kind of "special home," and forgot all about him. But she didn't! She knew she had made a commitment to him for life. She has stayed by his side faithfully for years as he has remained in this disabled condition—not because it was best for her, but because she loved her husband with an *unselfish* love, covenant love.

4. The world sees love as TEMPORARY; covenant love is LIFELONG.

When I was in the dating scene, many people told me, "Dating is the best preparation for marriage." For a while I believed that statement, but then I got to thinking about it.

How can dating prepare me for marriage? It's all based on temporary relationships: I see someone I like, I start a relationship, I get tired of him, I see someone else, I end the first relationship and start the next one. In the dating scene, I'd go from one temporary relationship to the next. If a relationship wasn't working, there was always an easy solution . . . break up and find someone new.

I finally came to the conclusion that dating was actually preparing me *not* for marriage . . . but for DIVORCE. It was teaching me to casually jump into a relationship and just end it whenever I felt like it. This is NOT the mind-set to take into a marriage that we expect to last a lifetime.

God created marriages to stand the test of time. You want a "happily ever after" love story? You can have one! Start today, by loving your future spouse with a COVENANT love . . . God's love. Get busy . . . you have a LOVE LIFE right now!

Love is patient, love is kind.
It does not envy, it does not boast,
it is not proud. It is not rude, it is not self-seeking,
it is not easily angered,
it keeps no records of wrongs.
Love does not delight in evil, but rejoices with the truth.
It always protects, always trusts, always hopes,
always perseveres.

Love never fails.
1 Corinthians 13:4–8 NIV

Lord, I choose to love my future spouse with covenant love instead of the world's shallow love. Help me view marriage, from now on, as a lifelong commitment. Help me remain faithful now to my future spouse so that I will lay the foundation for faithfulness after our marriage. Help me to learn to value what You value in a relationship—the eternal things. Cleanse my mind from the world's way of thinking. Teach me how to love . . . with agape love. Help me learn to think more of my future spouse than of myself. Teach me what covenant love is all about.

Broken Bread and Poured Out Wine
Eric and Leslie Ludy

It's but a shadow of His grace,
of His love it's but a taste;
The joining in covenant of two devoted lives—
a bridegroom and his bride.
It's a life of servanthood, out of love to show them good.
Humble dedication the washing of their feet;
That's what covenant really means.

All I have and all I am; giving my life.
Withholding not but sharing all;
Broken bread and poured out wine.

Remember Christ our King, His eternal offering.
He displayed his heart of love and grace,
Blood streaming down His beaten face.
He proposed to His beloved Bride,
With His very blood, His very life . . .

All I have and all I am; giving my life.
Withholding not but sharing all;
Broken bread and poured out wine.

Everything is looking just great on your castle! We really want to commend you for all the work that has gone into it. You must be so excited by now that you're ready to move in, right? There's only one problem—you have no roof! If you slept inside a castle without a covering, who knows what horrible things might happen . . . like getting rained on in the middle of the night, or maybe even receiving a lovely gift from one of the birds flying overhead—right on your face! Yuck! Better get out your hammer and nails.

STEP 5: Add the roof. Translated into relationships that means—

embracing the family.

Chapter 11
A Secret Key to Romance

Eric & Leslie

*P*icture it! There you are strolling along the beach with your wife-to-be. The setting is perfect! A warm summer breeze tickles your faces, the waves crash gently against the rocks, a seagull calls overhead, children giggle in the distance. The two of you stop and sit on a bench to gaze at the brilliant sunset that lights the sky over the ocean.

You sigh happily and turn to look into her eyes. Nothing can spoil this moment. You take a deep breath and begin to ask her that question you've been wanting to for so long.

"Susan, there's . . . something I want to ask you," you begin hesitantly.

"Yes?" she looks at you expectantly.

With trembling hand, you reach behind you and pull out a little white box. The moment you've been waiting for has finally arrived. Romance is in the air! Everything is beautiful! You just know that this is going to be the most perfect proposal that ever was. You open your mouth to speak to her, when suddenly you hear another voice from somewhere behind you . . .

"Hey, you two love birds!" blares your mother's voice over your shoulder. "Isn't this a great sunset? Wow! Look at those colors! Oh, Stevie! You have a ring! How romantic!"

Soon your dad pipes in, "Hey! Anybody want some popcorn?"

"We just couldn't miss the big moment!" chimes in your mother as she gets her camera out of her purse. "We wanted to be here to take a picture of when Susan agrees to marry you! This is just so exciting!"

You freeze. The romantic dream has turned into a nightmare! Your parents are following you wherever you go!

Your mouth goes dry and a knot forms in your stomach.

"Hey, Stevie, what are you waiting for?" belts out still another eerily familiar voice. "Ask her the question! I'm getting this all on video tape! Hey, your face is beat red! Did you use that cologne that you're allergic to again? Boy, does that stuff stink!"

You slowly turn around to come face to face with a video camera and a short person standing behind it. Your little brother! Ahhh!! Nooooo!!!

You jump up and run as fast as you can. You have to get away from your family! They are ruining everything! You don't look back; you just keep running. Your hear their voices faintly in the distance . . .

"Stevie! Where are you going?" demands Susan. "Don't leave me with these people! Help!"

"Hey, Stevie?" taunts your brother. "What's the matter? Do you have to go to the bathroom or something?"

"Why Stevie Smith!" yells your mother indignantly, "Come right back here, young man, and propose to Susan!"

Your life is over. Nothing will ever be right again! Romance is a thing of the past, and all because you went to that crazy seminar with Eric and Leslie Ludy. They told you to let your family be a part of your relationship with your future spouse. They ruined your life! You'll never get married, Susan will never speak to you again, everything is a disaster, you're destined to become a hermit forevermore . . . all because of them! You begin to seriously consider pressing charges.

Okay, okay, calm down. It's just a scenario; it's *not* reality! Whew! They could have made that scene into a horror movie!

♡ ♡ ♡

When we begin to hear phrases such as "embracing your family," visions of that awful situation on the beach begin to dance around in our minds. Letting our family be involved in this sacred area of our lives . . . relationships . . . sounds about as terrible as anything we can imagine. I mean, letting God have control of it was bad enough! Now, letting my *family* be a part of it?! NO WAY!

We are just positive they will mess it up, destroy the romance, and in every other way make the whole relationship one big depressing nightmare.

Well, let us both acknowledge that we UNDERSTAND *exactly* how you feel. Both Eric and I love our families, but the thought of having them be intimately involved in our future relationship would have made us run the other way! But we discovered by accident that involving our families was a secret key to romance in our relationship. Yes, you did read that right . . . romance!

We do not regret for a moment that our families were a big part of our relationship. Looking back, we realize they were a HUGE part of the beauty and romance we experienced in doing things God's way.

Eric and I had always desired to fall in love with and marry our best friend someday. It had always sounded like such a romantic experience to have a beautiful friendship with someone and then gently realize you were in love with each other.

As I grew older and went through the dating scene, I decided *that* hope was probably not a very realistic desire. I mean, how are you possibly supposed to become "best friends" with someone of the opposite sex when you are always trying to impress each other?

I would see a good-looking guy at school or at a party.

We'd exchange glances for a while. Pretty soon we'd be talking and flirting, and then next thing we knew, we'd be in a dating relationship. From the start, our relationship was based on nothing more than attraction to each other. I was never able to get "real" enough with a guy—past all the flirting and impressing—to actually consider him a true friend. *Dating always got in the way of creating true friendships.*

I met Eric during a time in my life when I had decided to give up dating relationships and focus on God until he brought my future husband across my path someday. Eric was five years older than me, and I considered him an older brother in the Lord.

The time we spent together when we were first getting to know each other was usually with our families. We would have family prayer meetings at each other's houses, picnics and barbecues, and many other times of fellowship. We even went on mission trips together as families!

Eric was probably the first young man that actually got to know me as I truly was. Why? Because our friendship grew while we were with our families. There was no way I could put on a false front to impress Eric in that setting! Especially with not one, but TWO younger brothers around to keep me humble! Brothers, sisters, and parents don't let you get away with anything!

It can seem like a major pain to think of getting to know someone in this way, but it was the best thing we could have done! After a few months of getting to know each other "as we really were," we realized we had quickly become true friends.

When God eventually began to show us that He meant us to be "more than friends," our families were able to fully embrace the new relationship and support it because they had

all been a part of watching it grow and develop. Our parents were thrilled at what God had done between us and gave us their full blessing to deepen our relationship. They trusted us! They were free to release us to be led by God in our relationship, because they had been a part of seeing God put it together.

Thoughts from Eric on Family

The words *family* and *romance* were never synonymous in my brain growing up. Family was associated with the dinner table, discipline, church, and a clean room. Romance was always associated with sweet nothings, stolen kisses, and drive-in movies. To say both words in the same sentence would have been like heaping salt on a hot fudge sundae. That is, until I began to realize God's way of doing things.

I actually stumbled into it. It was a Sunday afternoon in the middle of the summer of 1992. I went out to lunch with a man named Richard R. Runkles. Dum-da-dum . . . Leslie's father!

"Uhhh, Rich?" I muttered while wiping my sweaty palms on my napkin. "I think God has shown me that one day Leslie will be my wife!"

If I were to rank the most difficult sentences I've ever uttered in my life, that would probably rank as the second most heinous behind telling my brother, when he was four, that he had a birthmark on his backside. (Just kidding Marky!) There is something terribly awkward and unusual about saying something like that to a father. It's sort of like giving an important speech while your zipper is down. No matter how credible you try to sound, fathers can see right through you!

When I finally gasped out those fateful words, Rich

responded with the most extraordinary statement I may have ever heard in my life. "Eric," he said, "Janet and I have been praying for Leslie's future husband for fourteen years (that was when they became Christians), and we have known for quite some time that *you* are the one."

Now it's important to note that this wasn't our first conversation. I had previously come to Rich to gain counsel on how I could gently pull away from my relationship with his daughter so that we wouldn't be distracted from God's purposes for our lives. He had blessed me, at the time, to pursue a relationship with Leslie in any way God might lead me.

I hadn't realized how significant his statement was, but in the weeks that followed, God began to speak to me. He showed me that He had indeed been orchestrating my relationship with Leslie, and, in fact, had destined our lives to be together. Instead of going straight to Leslie with this exhilarating news, however, I had learned a different approach.

God had granted me eyes to see that there was a "bubble" around Leslie—a door that no one could enter unless he had the key. And there was only one man who held the key that was needed to enter the "bubble" surrounding this young lady . . . Rich Runkles, her father, the man who knew her better than any man on earth. So I went to him first. And that memorable morning as I sat sweating across the table from him . . . he handed me the key!

Even now that I had "the key," I didn't run straight to tell Leslie the news. Instead, I arranged a time that Rich and my own father and I could get together and talk. I wanted to do this right, and I knew that the prayer and counsel of "my two dads" was the safest way to make sure that I did.

Rich and my dad prayed for me and blessed the

relationship that was about to begin. Then Rich uttered the words I'll never forget, "Eric, I give you my blessing to win my daughter's heart."

It was at that moment this truth became vividly clear to me: "With the blessing of the father, comes the blessing of Heaven." Leslie was Rich's precious treasure, his responsibility to guard and protect until her husband took the role. By honoring his position as her father, God honored me. Our relationship was birthed in the right and proper order, and we have reaped the benefits ever since.

Over the months that followed, I began to meet with Rich on a regular basis. He knew Leslie better than anyone—at least from a man's perspective—and he began to instruct me on who she was and what her needs were. I learned more about how to be sensitive to Leslie from those talks with Rich than I ever could have from just relating with her.

Now, Back to Leslie . . .

When I found out that my parents had been feeling for many months that Eric was the man for me, and also that *his* parents were in total agreement, it was exactly the confirmation I needed to understand God's will. I had been feeling that way about Eric, but wanted God to show me through someone else. He chose that "someone else" to be our parents!

As Eric began meeting with my dad, I felt so honored. Here were two men—the two most important men in my life—meeting together for the sole purpose of talking about . . . ME! They discussed how to treat me and be sensitive to me and what my needs and desires were. What girl in her right mind wouldn't feel like a princess under such circumstances!

Not long after Eric spoke to my dad for the second time about our relationship, we got together as families—

all ten of us—to talk about what God was doing. We went around the room and every single person in each family— our brothers, sister, and parents—shared how God had revealed to them personally that our relationship truly was right. What an incredible night!

That day our families bonded together in a close-knit way. We have been the best of friends ever since. They were able to see our relationship grow and blossom into all God intended it to be. Of course, our families weren't perfect, and all of us made mistakes. But God still kept the love alive between us all. Throughout our relationship, Eric and I had the full blessing and support of each member of our families. Surely this was the way God intended it to be!

Not everyone has parents or family members who are in tune to God like ours were. Not everyone will be blessed with the kind of family we've been blessed with. But we firmly believe that God still has a remarkable plan for this area of each person's life. If you do all you can to honor the parents, brothers, and sisters God has given you, you can be sure God will give you a blessing you never could have experienced otherwise.

One of the most unforgettable moments I've ever experienced was just after our wedding ceremony. Eric and I, along with all of our family, met in a little room at the back of the church. Everyone was hugging and crying and laughing—all at the same time! It was beautiful! Our entire family felt as much a part of the celebration as we did! To begin a new life together with the full support and blessing and enthusiasm of our family was unbelievably uplifting and freeing! We were able to look ahead to our future with excitement and back at our past without regrets.

"Honor your father and mother"—
which is the first commandment with a promise—
"that it may go well with you
and that you may enjoy long life on the earth."
Ephesians 6:2–3 NIV

Lord, thank You for the family You've given me. Help me to always remember that they will never be perfect—that they will let me down because they are human, just like me. Help me to have the grace and strength to forgive my family where they have hurt me. I want to get past the pride and bitterness I feel towards them and start treating them with the love and respect You desire me to.

I want to discover Your plan in my family. Please give me the courage to invite their counsel and insight into my life. Give me the humility to listen to them, and the wisdom to take them seriously.

Break down the walls between us. Help me to love them unconditionally!

Okay, you've got the roof on—now you can move in! Yea! But wait a minute, aren't you missing something?

Walk into your castle for a minute. Sure, you've laid some great concrete and stone building blocks. There is even a rain and bird-dropping-proof ceiling up top. But how long will you want to stay in a place that has no carpet and no furniture—not to mention no heat?

Your castle needs what some would refer to as "a woman's touch." But, it can be "a man's touch," too. In fact, that's what this next chapter is all about, so guys . . . listen up and get out the decorating manual!

STEP 6: Add the carpet, furniture, and the fire in the fireplace. Translated into relationships that means—

tenderness.

Chapter 12
More than Flowers

Eric

*I*f we stopped now in the construction of our castle, we would have a brilliant structure capable of standing for hundreds, even thousands of years. It would laugh in the face of a storm and mock the encroaching tides. Yet, though it would stand with an iron-will, it wouldn't be too comfortable to live in. It would be nothing but a great big structure full of concrete walls and colorless halls, frigid floors, and protruding two-by-fours. It needs a little spice, a little color, maybe even a little back ground music. With the simple addition of carpeting, furniture, and a fire in the hearth, the entire atmosphere is changed.

What could that addition possibly be in a relationship? Hey! All you young single men out there, listen up! I would like to give you a little secret to winning a woman's heart.

We have all been told that women are fond of mink coats, diamond rings, bulging muscles, and, of course, hairy chests. Well, if that were true, I would still be single! Now I'm not here to say those qualities do *not* woo a woman's heart. But I'm here to say that there is another quality in a man that will beat a dozen roses hands down and huge biceps any day of the week.

Treating a woman *tenderly* is the greatest romance secret of all. It's this very tenderness that adds the carpeting, furniture, and fire to your castle of dreams.

Guys, I don't know if you've realized this yet, but tenderness isn't the most natural quality of us men. Where being tender would be comparative to a soft mattress, most of us are naturally a bed of nails. In our culture, softness and sensitivity are not valued as highly as being macho and muscle-bound. We men are taught to be tough and not show emotion—to be strong and never let 'em see us sweat. Yet, if we are going to truly be like Christ, we must learn to be gentle, sensitive, and tender.

Tenderness is an art! It involves forgetting about yourself and thinking about the needs of someone else. We are so conditioned to think only about ourselves. As a result, we oftentimes miss out on the beautiful fruit that tenderness bears. Imagine if Leslie accidentally got mustard all over my favorite shirt. When she realized what she had done, she would be mortified just thinking she was going to have to tell me. When she finally confessed the horrible deed, I'd have two choices of how to respond: *selfishly* or *tenderly*.

Responding selfishly would be to think about what life is going to be like without my Tommy Hilfiger rugby. Responding tenderly involves the simple act of looking at it from her perspective. Did she do it on purpose? Of course not! How does she need me to respond to her? She needs me to wrap my arm around her shoulder, kiss her on the cheek, and say, "Les, it's no big deal! I love you!"

Tenderness is the art of recognizing what someone else needs and acting accordingly. When I respond with tenderness, Leslie responds toward *me* with tenderness. The opposite also seems to be true as well. If I respond selfishly, it often stimulates a selfish response in return.

If I know that Leslie just needs to be held, tenderness would not try and make sense of *why* she needs to be held. It simply sees the need and responds. If I realize that Leslie is just sick and tired of being cooped up in the house, instead of reasoning that we went out to dinner last month, tenderness sees the need and creatively and ambitiously attempts to meet it.

There are even times when Leslie just needs to know that I am thinking about her throughout the day. Tenderness finds ways to express love in creative ways that are meaningful and full of surprises. A rosebud, a card, a dinner out—these are all ways that can creatively show tenderness and express love.

"That's great, Eric, but I'm not married! In fact, I don't even have a clue who I will marry! How can I learn tenderness without a marriage partner?"

That's a great question! You see, tenderness is not only something we express to our spouse when we get married, it's an attribute of Christ that we must learn to express to the world around us.

I wouldn't recommend giving a dozen roses to the mechanic down the road when you realize he's having a bad day! No, you need to recognize what would be special for *him*. Maybe he needs a thank-you note expressing how grateful you are that you found a mechanic as conscientious and as *inexpensive* as him.

Wrapping your arms around your dad's secretary, whispering sweet nothings in your neighbor's ear, and taking your third grade teacher out for a romantic dinner, are *not* advisable ways of practicing the art of tenderness. But try telling your mom how much you love her and her cooking. Share with your sister how good of a dancer she is and how proud you are to be in the same family with her. Give your brother a big hug, and let him know that he's the best brother in the whole world. You could even go to the store and purchase one of those "#1 Dad" tee-shirts and present it to your unsuspecting father. Okay, I didn't say learning tenderness would be easy!

Tenderness is not something that you will just develop when you get married. It is a trait that must be cultivated when you are young and pliable. At least it's a whole lot easier then. It may seem like it will be a piece of cake to express tenderness to your future spouse. In fact, it probably sounds a whole lot simpler to be tender with someone special in the future than to be tender with your biological family in the here and now.

My mom once told me, "Eric, the way you treat me is the way you will treat your wife!" I didn't believe it for a second. But as mothers always are, she was right. Where I was rude and insensitive with her, I would surely be rude and insensitive with the one I vowed to love and cherish.

God gave me the opportunity to reconcile the relationships with my family before I was married. Over a three year period I was able to practice tenderness on my mother and sister. No, it wasn't as thrilling as practicing on Leslie, but it was just as fulfilling. Tenderness is a beautiful salve on the heartaches of life. It adds a sparkle and a shine to the mundane, causing the frown to turn upside down.

This may sound like a betrayal to the male gender, but there have been times in my life when *I* just needed to be held and *I* just needed someone to be tender with me. When I was twenty-three, my mother held me on her lap like a little child and I wept in her arms. There was healing that needed to take place between us, and that one expression of tenderness broke through years of hurt and pride.

There have been quite a few times in our marriage when I have just needed Les to hold me and comfort me. In other words, ladies, men need to be treated with tenderness as well.

The words that Leslie speaks to me have a tremendous effect on my life. Because she knows me so well, she could destroy me with the words she speaks. Instead she has chosen to speak words that ennoble me and embolden me like a prince. She knows my every weakness, but she chooses to encourage me instead of tear me down. So if

you see me walking around with my shoulders back and a glimmer of confidence in my eye, you'll know Leslie has been speaking tenderly to me, encouraging me, making me a prince with her words.

The same is true in reverse. Leslie is very sensitive to the words I speak. I have the power in my words to either destroy her or mold her into a radiant princess. Tenderness is not just a nice tool to have in your future relationship, it's an essential tool. It's the difference of concrete walls and colorful halls.

Start now! Guys, go find your mother and tell her she's beautiful. Girls, track down your dad and let him know he's handsome and strong. Just watch what happens!

Do nothing from selfishness or empty conceit,
but with humility of mind
let each of you regard one another
as more important than himself;
do not merely look out for your own personal interests,
but also for the interests of others.
Philippians 2:3–4 NASB

Lord, forgive me for not being tender. Forgive me for living selfishly and considering my own needs above those of others in my life. Help me prepare for my future spouse by showing tenderness to my family and those in my community. Show me creative ways I can reach out beyond my own little world and love others. I want to be like You. Tenderize me. Soften my heart.

More than Flowers

Eric Ludy

With a sweet and tender rose and its delicate petals,
Your pretty face would yield a warm and radiant glow.
With flowers I could speak my heart, my love so deep,
But how much more importantly . . .

That you see me living out my love for you daily,
That you hear me adorning you with every word I speak,
That you catch me serving you in ways
you're not supposed to see.
Then you'll know . . . far more than flowers could ever show.

With a diamond cut so clear, set in gold to grace your ear,
I could charm your precious heart, win from your eyes a tear.
With gifts and costly stones, I could gain your heart as home,
But how much more importantly . . .

That you see me living out my love for you daily,
That you hear me adorning you with every word I speak,
That you catch me serving you in ways
you're not supposed to see.
Then you'll know . . . far more than flowers could ever show.

The world does not boast of tenderhearted men,
But I choose to live my life for the applause of Heaven.

Chapter 13
Do Knights in Shining Armor Really Exist?

Leslie

FOR GIRLS ONLY

*G*irls, here's a chapter written especially for you. (Guys, don't try to fool me! I know you're sneaking a peak at this chapter too, but let me warn you: *You read this at your own risk!* We are about to embark on to some serious "girl talk." If you think you're man enough to handle it . . . read on!) Now, where was I? Oh yes, back to the girls . . .

There she stands, her golden locks flowing about her shoulders, her snowy white gown billowing in the breeze. She looks over the stone wall down into the valley below. She sighs wistfully. In just a few hours the evil Count Hawkings will send her to her death. That is unless . . .

She hardly dares to hope that someone might rescue her. That would be nearly impossible! No one is smart enough or brave enough to out-scheme the Count.

Wait! What's that she hears in the distance? Galloping horse hooves? She lifts her eyes toward the sound. She gasps in surprise.

There, riding toward the fortress on a silvery white horse, is the most brave and handsome knight she has ever seen! He is galloping full speed ahead, apparently unafraid of the Count's mighty brigade of guards surrounding the fortress.

She watches in amazement as he disarms all fifty soldiers with one swipe of his sword. A second later he bursts through the door of the castle, and she can hear alarmed voices shouting below. After a brief scuffle, she hears footsteps charging up the stairs toward the room where she is locked in. A voice calls to her, "Stand back, my lady, I'm breaking down the door!" And in a moment, the noble knight is standing before her.

"You have rescued me!" exclaims the princess in delighted surprise.

"It was nothing," he replies humbly, taking her into his arms. He sweeps her up, carries her down the stairs past the bodies of the men he has singlehandedly defeated, places her on his silvery white horse, and they gallop away into the sunset. And they lived happily ever after . . . of course! *The End.*

♡ ♡ ♡

Do we have any guys still with us after a story like that? Well, I just told it to see how many of you were actually going to stick it out in this chapter. Just kidding! I have a VERY important reason for sharing this story.

Girls, I know you are all drooling over the knight in that story and wish you could be the maiden in distress, right? Well, okay, maybe that's a little extreme, but I'm fairly sure that every girl out there has her own "knight in shining armor" that she dreams of meeting one day. It must be something every girl in the history of the world is born with, because I've never met a girl who wasn't hoping for Prince Charming.

It's time to ask that all important question . . . *Do knights in shining armor really exist?* I mean, it's one thing to read about them in the fairy tales, but what about in real life?

Throughout this book so far, we've been talking about saving yourself completely, physically, and emotionally for the man you will one day marry . . . waiting for God's BEST in a future husband. But I'll bet the question has run through your mind, *"Is he really out there?"* Not just anyone, but someone really worth waiting for! Someone you can really get excited about saving yourself for. Does someone like that exist?

"Sure," you tell me, "I've read your and Eric's love story. Eric is certainly a "knight in shining armor," but after living for eighteen years and meeting hundreds of guys, I can tell

you for sure that he is the *only one* alive on this earth . . . and he's already taken! So what do I have to look forward to?"

I grew up dreaming about my knight in shining armor. A man who was brave. A man who was strong, but most of all a man who was kind and gentle and sensitive . . . a man who treated me like a princess. I would tell my family all about this man and how I would settle for nothing less than a prince charming. When I would see movies on TV where the hero fell short of the "prince-charming" standard, I would roll my eyes and wonder how the heroine could even put up with him.

"It's going to take a very special man to win your heart," my dad would comment with a smile. I would grin back with confidence. I knew he was out there somewhere! My daydreams were full of this man sweeping me off my feet as soft, melodious music played in the background.

Time went on and I kept on dreaming and believing that my knight would come knocking on my door one day. And then . . . I went to high school. (Lovely music abruptly stops and switches to an obnoxious bus horn sound!)

I took one look around at the guys, and all my starry-eyed ideals fell down with a loud thud. There was not even *one* who came close to fitting my "knight in shining armor" standard.

Brave? Ha, what a joke! I could see right through their "hot-shot" stance and cool clothes. They were as insecure as they could possibly get.

Gentle? Give me a break! None of them had one inkling of a clue how to treat a woman. No manners whatsoever! They would push us and shove us, spit on our shoes and make fun of us, and tell the most disgusting jokes they could think of.

Sensitive? Let's just say I think that was a foreign word to them. They were so far gone they couldn't even DEFINE the word sensitive!

One memorable evening I was chatting on the phone with Johnny (remember him from the second chapter?) and we were running out of things to talk about.

"I know!" he suggested. "Bret is over at David's tonight. Let me call them up on a three-way, and I won't tell them you're on the line. Then you can listen to a 'guy' conversation!"

It sounded interesting enough, so I agreed. Soon I was listening to the three of them talk. Within the first five minutes, I was so repulsed I couldn't have spoken if I wanted to!

These guys were talking in the most perverted, derogatory way about MY friends! They were describing these girls' bodies and discussing them as if they were *pieces of meat!* These three guys were not rebels, or drop-outs, or druggies, or hippie-wanna-be's. They were guys who went to church, made good grades, played sports, and were part of the popular crowd. They were the best of the guys to choose from, and even they fell SO FAR away from the standard I held in regard to "a knight in shining armor." I was furious!

Once Johnny had gotten them off the phone he asked, "Well, how did you like it?"

"Is THAT how you talk about GIRLS?!" I fumed.

"Sure, what's wrong with it?" he wanted to know.

Never mind, you egotistical insensitive jerk! I thought to myself. I knew he would never understand.

Needless to say, my confidence in finding a "knight in shining armor" began to seriously wane. In fact, as my high school days slipped by, I decided that I would be lucky even to end up with a man who *didn't* treat me like a piece of

meat. So I began to lower my standards. I dated guys I would *never* have wanted to marry. Even my desire to "save myself" for my husband began to become weaker, simply because I thought that he wouldn't be worth it if he was anything like the guys I was surrounded with.

Obviously, that's NOT the way the story ends, though! Girls, you already know that God *did* bring me a "knight in shining armor." But how did I get to the point of almost giving up believing he was out there to having him come into my life?

Well, God didn't let me give up. As He began to work on my heart and gain control of this area of my life, He began to show me that I shouldn't be lowering my standards in men and running from one relationship to the next, desperately hoping to find this "knight." Instead, I should be waiting for Him to bring that man to me—trusting that He really would bring me someone worth waiting for.

I realized that it wasn't just "prince charming" I wanted in a man, it was the *character of Jesus Christ!* Think about it! Why are "knights in shining armor" so appealing to us as women? Because they are all the things Christ is—caring, kind, gentle, sensitive, brave, noble . . . the list goes on. And Jesus is the Perfect Gentleman. There is no other man that understands how to treat a woman like a princess better than Jesus. So instead of looking for "prince charming," I began to look for "the character of Christ" in a husband.

Have you, like me, ever doubted that men like this exist? Or that there is one man like this out there just for you? It's VERY hard to keep believing as we are surrounded by guys who are SO FAR from being godly. But Satan *wants* us to stop believing that our man is out there. He wants us to stop

having standards. He doesn't want us to have someone worth waiting for. He would *love* for every girl to settle for less than a "knight in shining armor." Why? Because he knows that when God brings two people together that have set themselves apart for each other in absolute purity, the result is a strong and beautiful marriage, which results in a strong and beautiful family, which results in people who change this world for Christ.

Girls, I want to be completely honest with you . . . Satan is *working overtime* trying to get you to throw away your treasure, both inward and outward. He will do everything in his power to get you to lower your standards, to give up waiting for that "special" someone. That's why you've GOT to know where you stand.

There is a story about a secretary and her boss, sitting in the office one day having a little conversation. It goes something like this:

Boss: Hey, babe, would you sleep with me for a million dollars?

Lady: A million dollars?!?! Sure!

Boss: Okay, how about for five dollars?

Lady: Five dollars?! No way! What kind of a woman do you think I am?!

Boss: We've already decided that, now we're just negotiating price.

Ouch! That hurts, especially if you are one of the many girls who would have responded the very same way. If we are going to discover God's beautiful plan for us in the area of romance, we must first understand how valuable the treasure God has given us is. There is NO PRICE worth giving away that treasure for.

We've got to be committed to Jesus in such a passionate way that our response is always, "I belong to Jesus Christ. I want His highest for my life. Even a million dollars could never satisfy me the way His perfect plan will. I love Him, and giving myself away would break His heart. I trust that He has a plan for me; I *cannot* lower my standards."

It's a constant battle! You *must* know where you stand. The first time I was seriously asked to have sex with a guy, I was just thirteen years old! For some, it is even younger. Fortunately, I knew where I stood and I said no. But the pull and pressure from guys to give away our treasure, whether it's physically or emotionally, only gets worse as we get older.

Our society has gotten to the place where it is the cool thing to be "loose." It's not cool to have high standards. You have a choice. You can give in, sacrifice a precious treasure, and taint the beautiful plan God has for you and your "knight" someday. Of course you'll look "cool" and have a good time—at least for a while. Or, you can sacrifice the temporary pleasures of today and allow God to paint the most romantic love story ever written—in your life!

When your knight in shining armor finally comes to sweep you off your feet, you will have a pure and priceless treasure to give him . . . and believe me it's well worth the wait!

A young girl recently told me a situation she'd gone through with a young man.

"This guy asked me out. I was really torn because I like him a lot, but I didn't feel God wanted me in the relationship. So I said no. A few weeks later, he started dating my friend. Now I feel disappointed, like I gave up an opportunity or missed out on something."

My response was this: "Why would you want to waste your time and energy and affection on someone who

obviously didn't love you wholly and completely? The reason he asked you out was because he wanted a girlfriend. You were obviously his first choice, but when that fell through, he went to your friend instead. Why would you even want to be in a relationship with someone who just wants a girlfriend?"

We have to face the facts, girls (and guys, for those of you who are still with us) . . . most guys are simply not an example of Christ. Most of the guys we see today are not the kind worth saving our treasure for. Usually they will charm us a little and take part of our treasure (whether it be physical or emotional) and use it for their own benefit. They are selfish. We shouldn't give that treasure to *anyone* who is using us. Our treasure is meant only for someone who will love us and be committed to us with his whole heart . . . not someone who just wants a girlfriend!

It's easy to want to settle for less than God's best for you. Even if he's not a complete "jerk," he still may not be God's very highest. Many girls will latch on to the first guy that shows interest in them simply because they think if they don't, they will miss their only chance for a relationship. Satan would love to see you make this mistake. Remember, the enemy of the BEST is often the GOOD! Sure, the guy you are settling for may be a nice guy. He may even be a Christian. He may look great next to you and have a last name that you'd love to carry around, but don't forget to ask the key question: Is he God's BEST for my life?

The second most important decision you will ever make is who you decide to marry. (It's second only to your decision to follow Christ.) It's not something you want to take lightly. So many women tell us, "Oh, how I wish I had done things differently! My whole life would have turned out better!"

Picture this scenario: A young woman, eager to be in a relationship, began dating a man who was charming but a little on the distrustful side. She was enthralled with him simply because he flattered her and was attracted to her. Her parents could see right through him and warned her not to date him, but she stubbornly remained in the relationship, determined not to lose him. She knew he had some problems, but she was sure he would change. She just didn't want to live without his love.

They eventually became engaged. Her parents and even her friends urged her all the stronger NOT to marry him. She didn't listen. Just before her wedding, however, she was suddenly struck with the horrifying realization that she was about to marry the wrong person. But because she was afraid she would never have another chance to marry, she went ahead with the wedding.

Just a few years later this "charmer" walked out on her, never to be seen again, taking the majority of her assets and leaving her with three small children to raise on her own. Her life has been full of trials and struggles ever since.

This scenario is sad, but common. Don't make the same mistake she did. Never be tempted to settle for less than God's BEST for your life.

It's also important to realize that even if you have blown it, even if you have given away that precious treasure, God can restore it and make it beautiful again. We all make plenty of mistakes. The important thing is, once we realize where we've gone wrong, to do all we can to make it right, then turn and go the other way. God STILL has a beautiful plan for you. He is very capable of taking what Satan meant for your destruction and using it for His glory! And He will do just that, if you simply trust Him.

When I realized how much I had lowered my standards and how much of my treasure I'd given away foolishly, I was grieved. I couldn't imagine how God could still bless me with a "knight in shining armor" now. It was right about that time God brought three or four young men into my life who were different from the kind of guys I was used to. They weren't flirtatious or perverted or stuck on themselves. They were sold out to Jesus! He was the number one focus of their lives. And I became friends with all of them.

They amazed me. For the first time I was actually able to have pure, godly friendships with members of the opposite sex. Our time spent together centered around God and what He was doing in each of our lives. They were like older brothers to me. I saw that God had placed them in my life for a very special reason. Not for me to rush out and marry one of them, but to show me that He did, indeed, have a man, just like one of these young men, out there for me. I felt unworthy.

You might also feel unworthy of such a gift. But there's nothing wrong with feeling unworthy . . . because we ARE unworthy. We HAVE blown it, but God is so merciful. It's time to rise up to be the kind of women He has called us to be, to take our stand, and to trust in His beautiful plan for each one of us.

No matter what your situation, no matter where you've been, how smart you are or what you look like, if God's will for you is marriage, you can know that God *is* raising up a "knight in shining armor" just for you. Don't settle for ANYTHING LESS!

♡ ♡ ♡

Let me finish this chapter by sharing the paraphrased Ludy version of a story Max Lucado recently told in his

book, *The Angels Were Silent*. It's a true story that we can all learn from. The heroine in the story KNEW what she was waiting for in a man—true godly character—and she wasn't about to settle for just anyone!

A Truly Amazing Love Story

A tall, dashing soldier named John Blanchard went into a library one day and checked out a book. (I know that sounds like a really boring past-time, but he was probably just homesick and didn't know what else to do. Anyway, it led to something more exciting.) He came across some notes in the margins as he was reading. "Wow!" he thought to himself as he looked them over. "I'd really like to meet whoever wrote these notes. They are so insightful and inspiring!"

He found a name in the front of the book: Harlyss Maynell, New York City. (Yes, I know she has a weird name, but keep an open mind to her because she's an important character in this story.) The bright idea occurred to him that she was the person who wrote those notes in the margin! Then he did something rather crazy and impulsive, the kind of thing that ends up on one of those "top ten" lists that says you know you are lonely when . . . No. 1: You check out a library book, find a name in the inside cover, and give the person a call to ask them out on a date. Well, okay, John didn't ask Harylss on a date . . . but he did give her a call! He looked up her name in the New York City phone book and asked if they could start writing letters. (I guess that was before e-mail.)

That was a bold act, if I've ever seen one. This guy didn't even know Harlyss! For all he knew, she could be a drug-dealer, mafia member, or ax murderer! But he was willing to

take a chance. Doesn't it make you wonder about those notes in the margins? They must have been pretty inspiring, don't you think? Maybe John was desperate for a friend.

Anyway, back to Harlyss Maynell. She turned out to be a really terrific person. She must have taken a liking to John, because she agreed to write to him even though he was being shipped overseas to fight in the war. So they wrote for a while, and eventually John began to fall in love with Harlyss . . . even though he'd never seen her! He'd only seen what she'd written in her letters and in the margins of that library book. Nevertheless, he was smitten! (Girls, aren't you thinking right about now that you'd love to take writing lessons from Harlyss? Imagine, winning a man's heart through your pen! You'd never even have to wear make-up to do it! Just kidding!)

It must have started bothering John that he didn't know what Harlyss looked like, because he wrote her and asked her to send a picture of herself. But she firmly replied, "No, I will not send you a picture because relationships shouldn't be built upon looks." (Uh, oh. Guys, would you take this as a clue that maybe Harlyss isn't the best looking person in the world? Sure the girl can write, but what's wrong with her looks that she won't even send a picture?)

Many guys would have turned the other direction, right then and there. But John didn't. Like I said, her letters and book notes were incredible. So he must have told himself that she was just a woman of high ideals. He kept falling more in love with her even though he had no picture to put under his pillow. Imagine daydreaming about someone you'd never seen, but thought you loved?

Finally the chance came for John to meet Harlyss in person. He was coming back to the Sates for R & R, so he

wrote her and asked her to meet him somewhere so he could take her to dinner. She replied that she would meet him in New York City under the big clock. She said that he would recognize her by the fact that she'd be wearing a red rose.

So the day arrived, and there John stood under the clock, watching and waiting. He was just a little nervous. After all, this was no ordinary "first date." I mean, how would you feel if you had fallen in love with someone's handwriting and now were going to meet not just her hand, but her eyes and face? And what about that incident with the picture? Was there something about her that she hadn't wanted John to know? It was only moments before he found out.

A beautiful young woman began walking toward him, beckoning him to follow her with a provocative smile. For a brief moment, John thought he was looking at Harlyss. He could hardly believe his good fortune! Not only was she talented and a great writer, she was gorgeous! But then he realized she wasn't wearing a red rose. His heart sank with disappointment as she walked past him.

Suddenly he noticed a woman who was wearing a rose, standing there smiling up at him. He almost choked with despair. She was a homely woman, short and squatty, older than his mother, with grey hair sticking out under a well-worn hat. Her eyes twinkled pleasantly as she looked at him. He glanced back at the vanishing figure of the pretty young women feeling torn in two. (I'm sure that's an understatement. I mean, guys, what would you do in this situation? One guy I met told me if he was John Blanchard, he would have run straight back to the war and made sure he got shot!)

But John Blanchard turned out to be a hero. I'm glad,

because I'm starting to like John. He didn't run away, pass out, or act rudely. In fact, he realized that even though he could not have a love relationship with Harlyss, he could show gratitude to this woman who had truly befriended him through her letters. So he smiled (as well as he could at that horrible moment) and said to the plump woman, "Hi, you must be Harlyss Maynell. Thank you so much for coming to meet me. May I take you out to dinner?" (Now that was truly noble! How many guys do you know who would respond that way?)

The woman was surprised. She told him, "Son, I really don't know what all this is about, but remember that beautiful young lady that just passed you a moment ago? She told me to wear this rose in my coat and said that if you should ask me to dinner, she's waiting for you in the big restaurant across the street. She said it was some kind of test."

Wow! Can your emotions handle a story like that? Just when you had given up on Harlyss Maynell, she turns out to be talented, beautiful, and incredibly wise. She *knew* she didn't want to get in a relationship with a man who had no character. She knew that a man with character would place more value on the inside of a person, instead of just the outside. What a way to find out a man's character!

Girls, before you let yourself fall in love with anyone . . . put him to the test. You don't want to spend the rest of your life married to a whimp! John Blanchard proved himself worthy of Harlyss' time and attention. Don't settle for anyone less than a man who is worthy of *your* time and attention. Keep your standards high!

For those guys who have braved this entire chapter, congratulations. I'm sure you did not read this without a

little sweating and squirming. But I believe that even you can be changed into a "knight in shining armor" by God's grace! And you never know, one of the beautiful young ladies reading this right now just might be your princess someday . . . so you'd better get busy! She's got sky-high standards, and you know she's going to see right through you if you're not a true "knight!"

Many a man claims to have unfailing love,
but a faithful man who can find?
The righteous man leads a blameless life;
blessed are his children after him.
Proverbs 20:6 TLB

♡ ♡ ♡

Lord, I don't want to settle for anything less than Your best. Please help me stay strong, never swaying to the left or the right. Help me abide in You. Help me guard my heart against the men that may try to steal away my treasure. Keep me pure for my future husband. Help me wait for my knight in shining armor, Your best for me. Until You bring that man to me, don't let me be deceived by anyone else. Keep my eyes on You. Keep my standards high.

Wow! It's beautiful! You've been slaving and sweating over your castle and now it's finally finished! It's got everything—a solid foundation, a moat and drawbridge, a secluded piece of land, a secure roof overhead, and plush carpet on the floor. It's the kind of castle that will last forever. That is . . . IF you decide to keep it that way!

Yes, that's right—*you* are the one who gets to determine whether or not your castle stays looking its best or whether it becomes a dingy, dirty junk-heap someday. Castles are high-maintenance objects! Who wants a castle that, after a few hundred years, starts looking more like a haunted house?

Remember what it says at the end of every fairy tale? *They lived happily after!* The only way for that to happen is to keep your castle in mint condition.

The last and final step in this building process is . . . consistency! Translated into relationships that means *live out your commitments daily* . . for the rest of your life! If you do, you can be sure you'll have a "happily ever after" ending!

Chapter 14
Lights, Camera, Action!

Eric & Leslie

There is a challenging story we once heard about two Chinese Christian men who were put into a frigid prison cell for sharing their faith. They were in agonizing pain because of the bone-chilling cold, and they had only one thin blanket each to keep them warm.

One of the men looked at his Christian brother sitting next to him, shaking, and he asked himself, "If that were Jesus, would I give him my blanket?" As much as he could hardly stand the thought of parting with his only source of comfort, he realized that since Jesus had given *everything* for him, the least he could do would be to give everything he had in return, even though it was only a thin blanket. Out of his love and devotion to Jesus Christ, and gratitude for all Jesus had done for him, he sacrificially wrapped the thin piece of cloth around his friend's shoulders.

Quite a powerful story, right? So what does that have to do with your life? You may never find yourself in a freezing prison cell with nothing but a thin blanket, but you still have a similar choice to make. Selfish or *selfless*?

Think of your future spouse. Are you willing to give him or her your blanket? Maybe your blanket is ragged and torn. Maybe it has many holes in it, but you can still choose from this day forward to give your future spouse what you have. Your most priceless treasure . . . your purity, both internal and external. Your decision to wait for him or her.

Remember, it's not just about your own future. The choices you make today will affect your children's children!

Just think what could happen if we had a "purity revival" in the land and hundreds of couples were brought together God's way . . . with a sure foundation. Strong, lasting marriages would form, creating strong families to influence this world for Christ! What a revolution!

On the other hand, if we continue building relationships out of sand and cards without the sure foundation of Christ, how can we hope for strong marriages, strong families, or strong individuals who can change this world?

Even if you aren't called to be married, all of us are called to a life of purity. Each one of us needs to realize how much Jesus did for us and be willing to give him *everything* we have. Your commitment to living a life consistent with Christ's standard WILL change the world around you.

You may have been challenged and inspired to wait for God's best in your life as you have read this book. Now is the time to take the truth you've learned and put it into action! Now you must live out what you believe, day to day.

From this moment forward, are you willing to set yourself apart for that one special person? It's a daily choice. It won't be easy, but you can know that Jesus is right there beside you, cheering you on, encouraging you each step of the way. Will you give *your* blanket? You might think you'll freeze to death if you do, but nothing compares to the warmth of Jesus' radiant smile in return!

Imagine This . . .

All of Heaven was astir. There was an excited musical hum hanging over each angels' dwelling. "Praise be to God!" they called to each other happily as they passed on the golden streets. Everyone could feel that a fresh, new change was in the air. They had caught glimpses of the Creator's joyful glow and they knew something was happening down on earth. Something incredible. Something revolutionary. Something . . .

"Daa daa daaaaaa!" interrupted a piercing trumpet call. Seraphs and cherubs from everywhere began rushing toward

the sound. It was time for a meeting! They approached Michael who was grinning enthusiastically. Breathlessly they waited for him to speak.

"My friends!" his voice rang out. "Never before have we known a time such as this! There is a great awakening taking place among the children on earth. A revival such as never has been seen before! You will hardly believe your eyes!"

As he spoke, the gigantic screen began to drop and the angels took their seats, spellbound. The movie began to roll. The heavenly hosts gasped in awe. On the screen appeared hundreds, no . . . thousands, of young people from all over the world, on their knees, voicing their decision to set their lives aside in purity for their future spouse . . . their choice to wait for God's very best. The angels had rarely observed such resolve and fervor as what they now saw in the eyes of these youth. Surely this would change the course of history!

The picture altered. This time it showed young couples being supernaturally directed together by God. Love stories forming! And not just any love stories . . . PURE love stories! As the host of Heaven watched with rapt attention, they could clearly see the innocence and purity and *romance,* that was a classic mark of the Creator's loving hand, surrounding each of these young couples like a bubble. He was doing it! He was writing more beautiful romances! Each one so incredibly unique. Each one so right. Each one so full of the Great Director's heart.

An exultant cheer arose from the vast crowd. What awesome, wonderful news!

"Does this mean we will see more of the big screen from now on?" questioned a lovely seraph as the cheering died down.

Michael smiled. "Anyone in the mood for an all-night movie marathon?"

The angels trumpeted and laughed and applauded in joyful response.

He continued. "I am happy to announce that the leading roles of the Great Director's screenplays have all been accepted. And the best part is, there are still more to be written!"

As the angels sang and danced for joy, Michael quietly stepped aside to whisper something into his Master's ear. "They just can't go wrong when they discover *Romance God's Way*, can they?" he whispered.

The Great Director shook His head and smiled. Then beaming with a thoughtful, brilliant expression, He lifted His pen and began to write.

Dear reader, could it be YOUR love story He is writing next? Could you settle for anything less than one of His own glorious screenplays, handwritten just for you?

Take the truths you have found today, and put them into action! The Great Director is looking down on your life, and maybe a few angels with their bucket of popcorn are getting ready to pull out the big screen! It's YOUR turn to experience *Romance God's Way*! Put the pen in His hand and you will never be sorry you did!

Are you ready? Lights . . . camera . . . ACTION!!

Those who wait for the LORD
Will gain new strength;
They will mount up with wings like eagles,
They will run and not get tired,
They will walk and not become weary.
Isaiah 40:31 NASB

No Longer a Virgin?

~ Leslie ~

Believe me, you might think you're the only one of our readers taking time to look at this last, rather painful section of our book, but you're not. So many of us have blown it in this area! We've given ourselves away either emotionally or physically or both. We've lost that beautiful treasure. So what now? What do *you* do with these truths that you only wish you had put into action earlier? Can God *still* possibly have a plan for this area of your life? Can He even consider bringing you a "knight in shining armor" or a "princess of purity" after what you've done? Or is it just too late for you to experience *Romance God's Way?*

Consider this TRUE story from Jesus' days here on earth:

> Jesus returned to the Mount of Olives, but early the next morning he was back again at the Temple. A crowd soon gathered, and he sat down and talked to them. As he was speaking, the Jewish leaders and Pharisees brought a woman caught in adultery and placed her out in front of the staring crowd.
>
> "Teacher," they said to Jesus, "this woman was caught in the very act of adultery. Moses' law says to kill her. What about it?"
>
> They were trying to trap him into saying something they could use against him, but Jesus

stooped down and wrote in the dust with his finger. They kept demanding an answer, so he stood up again and said, "All right, hurl the stones at her until she dies. But only he who never sinned may throw the first!"

Then he stooped down again and wrote some more in the dust. And the Jewish leaders slipped away one by one, beginning with the eldest, until only Jesus was left in front of the crowd with the woman.

Then Jesus stood up again and said to her, "Where are your accusers? Didn't even one of them condemn you?"

"No, sir," she said.

And Jesus said, "Neither do I. Go and sin no more."[1]

Jesus was the only One in the entire crowd without sin. He could have condemned her. *He* could have been the one to throw the first stone. But He didn't. He forgave her. He spoke tenderly to her, as if she were a princess, yet she had just been caught in a horrible sin. Jesus loved her in spite of her weakness.

If you have fallen in this area of purity and you are truly repentant for what you have done, if you truly desire the healing and forgiveness of Jesus, He is waiting with open arms. He wants to wipe away those guilty stains sin has left upon your heart. All you have to do is ask and receive.

Lord Jesus, I have sinned. I have not lived up to Your standards in this area of purity. I have gone against Your perfect will for my life. Please forgive me. Only You can make me clean. Only You can give me a

fresh start. Take my broken, wounded heart, pick up the pieces, and help me start over. I thank You for the blood You shed which can cleanse me of this sin. I accept Your forgiveness now. Help me forgive myself. Help me live in purity from this day forward. Thank You.

As you pray a sincere prayer of repentance, Jesus will tenderly lift your chin and reply, "Neither do I condemn you. Now go your way, and sin no more."

Repentance literally means turning around and walking the OTHER direction. Where once you had been impure and sinful, Jesus now wants to make you white as snow! What was once your greatest weakness can now become your greatest strength, through the healing power of Christ!

He will not only forgive you, He will RESTORE you. Yes, there are consequences you must face because of your mistakes, but with His forgiveness, you can pick up the pieces and move on.

Never forget that He *still* has a beautiful plan for this area of your life! As you choose from this day forward to walk in purity and remain in His will, He will blow your mind with blessings! He is able to take this mistake in your life and turn it for good. If you trust Him and let Him have control from this day forward, You will be amazed at the divine plans that unfold before you.

Neither Eric nor I deserved the incredible, romantic, and pure relationship God granted us. We had made SO MANY mistakes! Before we met, both of us struggled with wondering if God would someday grant us a pure and strong relationship with someone we loved. We knew we didn't deserve it . . . we really didn't deserve to be married at all! But finally we realized that it wasn't about whether or not we were WORTHY of such a gift—none of us are

worthy of what Jesus gives us—but it was because of His LOVE and MERCY towards sinners like us.

From this day on, you are a new person! You can look ahead to the future with excitement and joy! Place your mutilated treasure into His ready hands, and just watch as He gives you a shiny new treasure in return. It's time to start over, this time, with Him by Your side.

[1] John 8:1–11 TLB.

White as Snow

Leslie Ludy

Alone and confused, your heart is bruised from sin.
Your joy is gone from love gone wrong,
Trying to start over again.

I know that you've been hurt, and you don't know who to
trust.
I won't pretend I understand your pain,
But I can see repentance in your eyes,
and I know it's not too late.
I hear Him calling your name . . .

White as snow, He has made you white as snow.
The moment you confessed, His heart forgave.
You might think you've ruined all the plans He had for you,
But it's for that very reason Jesus saves.
White as snow, He has made you white as snow,
Pure and innocent like a dove.
Though you have done nothing to deserve His pardoning,
You've been purified by Jesus' blood,
White as snow.

The guilt and the shame, keeping you chained,
Not wanting to let you go.
It's not how you dreamed, it's not how you planned.
You can't see that, still, there is hope.
Receive His healing for your bruises;
Receive His riches for your rags.
You cannot imagine all the plans He has for you,
So take His hand, and don't look back . . .

Resources Available

His Perfect Faithfulness—Eric and Leslie Ludy, $9.95
Don't miss this gripping account of a true love story built by God!

Romance God's Way—Eric and Leslie Ludy, $10.95
Fun, humorous and practical. Life-changing principles for young people in pre-marriage relationships.

Romance God's Way, **the video**—Eric and Leslie Ludy, $19.95
Filmed before a live audience, Eric and Leslie's dynamic seminar for youth and parents. Approx. 2 and l/2 hours.

Heavenly Perspective, **Music CD**—Eric and Leslie Ludy, $14.95
Original songs by Eric and Leslie. Full of worshipful, inspirational music to lead you into the presence of God.

To order
Contact Winston House Books
26897 Matthew Road
Parma, ID 83660
1-800-942-0177

To find out more
about the ministry of Eric and Leslie Ludy,
including booking information,
please contact:

R-Generation

P.O. Box 2225
Longmont, CO 80501
(303) 702-0177
E-mail: rgen@indra.com